Feel Good

Marriage

7 Steps to
a Rock Solid Relationship
Without Counseling

by Marko Petkovic

DEDICATED to my wife, Nathaly, my friend, closest ally and lover, who reached out her hand to me as together we started our journey transforming our relationship into the beautiful one that we have now. My dear wife and I found a way of understanding that has plainly transformed us, and the way we are for, and with, each other. We came so close to losing each other, and the preciousness of what we have now continues to floor us.

This book I also dedicate to my sons, Ziga and Nik, especially Nik who, in his own little way, showed us that we were doing something terribly wrong in our marriage, and unknowingly kicked us in the right direction.

I also need to acknowledge Irene, a teacher at Nik's kindergarten with a big heart and a warm soul, who unknowingly sparked the healing process of my marriage. When things were at their worst, she gently opened our eyes to the fact that we were about to screw up our youngest son if we didn't do something. As we started to "fix him", we discovered it was not our son who had to be fixed, but our relationship.   She   knew   that   from   the   beginning.

Contents

Preface

Any two people can have a marriage that lasts. What good, however, is a lasting marriage if the two people involved are unhappy? What good is a lasting marriage when partners feel uneasy around each other, or even emotionally threatened?

If you are anything like my wife and me, and I ask you how your marriage is, you probably won't say your marriage is a complete disaster, nor is it a marriage made in heaven. Most probably it would be somewhere in between.

Still, you know it's not okay. It's not what you want. Sometimes it feels more like you are business partners sharing the tasks of bringing home money, managing the housework and raising children. You're missing the bond you once had, and you want that feeling back.

This is the book for all of you who feel stuck in a not so good relationship and don't know how to make it better. Those who don't know what to do or how to do it, but believe in their relationships and don't want to quit. Not just yet.

This book is for couples who want to smile again when they think of each other. This book is for you, if you are interested in being best friends, allies, supporters, cheerleaders and lovers with your partner again.

This book is for couples who want to feel close, and emotionally and physically connected again, accepted, loved and adored for who they are.

This book is also for those of you who have, or are planning to have, children and you want them to grow up in a healthy emotional atmosphere. I can't emphasize that aspect enough. I believe the greatest gift that parents can give to their children is letting them experience firsthand their father cherishing their mother, and their mother adoring their father.

As you will discover later in the book, it was my children who made me realize that my wife and I were doing something wrong in our relationship. For now, let me just say, if you have trouble in your relationship and you don't do anything to resolve it, it's highly probable that your children will be repeating the very same mistakes as yours, as they will simply not know any better. This is another reason to act now.

This is also the book for those of you who might be thinking of divorce even if the idea has just crossed your mind. Maybe the word divorce has already been said out loud a couple of times. Thinking of your relationship, you might think that you just weren't lucky this time and you haven't found a perfect partner yet.

If you or your children are not being physically or emotionally abused or if there isn't a repeating pattern of drug or alcohol abuse, don't give up on your partner just yet. I strongly believe most couples in trouble need a bit of additional education, guidance, a lot of practice, but above all determination and persistence.

By the same token, isn't it funny that we get a user manual for almost anything, yet we get no instructions for how to make our relationships work?

Many people get divorced only to regret it a few years down the line. Once they get into another relationship, if the only thing they have changed is their partner, they often will face the same problems they had before. By the time they realize this, it's usually too late.

Remember, divorce is a permanent solution for a temporary problem.

If your spouse has moved out already, I am truly sorry. But don't despair. I believe that, even if things have gone this far, you can still repair your relationship. It may just take a bit longer.

Even if it's already too late, and divorce is behind you, if you are looking for a new relationship, then use this book to learn a new way of working within your relationships to avoid making the same mistakes over and over again. You just HAVE to know better for your next relationship, otherwise you will end up in the same trouble after a couple of years, maybe even sooner. It's okay to make mistakes, but only fools make exactly the same mistake twice. Odds are, if you continue using the same approach as you did in your previous relationship, (and obviously that wasn't so successful) you will do just that. It's your life and the only thing that can't be recovered is time. So why not begin using it properly and have a wonderful relationship next time?

Maybe you're wiser than the rest of us and you're reading this book before getting into any trouble. Maybe you're happy with things as they are now. Maybe you feel you're already in a great relationship, and you want to make it even greater. Maybe you're not in a relationship at this moment, but want to educate yourself before entering into one. I can only express my kudos to you. I truly admire you and I only wish I had this awareness when I entered into my relationship. It would without any doubt have saved us and my children quite some trouble.

Most of the stuff that you'll find in this book is common sense, when you think about it. But you have to think about it. On the other hand, things explained in this book are proven. They do magical things to people who have almost forgotten how to be nice and loving to each other. By applying the techniques and skills from this book, I was able to transform my marriage once the puzzle came together and we started doing the right things in the right order. This book is about that puzzle.

You can do it. You can make your relationship work because it's not rocket science. There is nothing mystical about it, but the results are magical.

As a matter of fact, you'll see the first results soon without having to wait for months with no sign of improvement. But the lasting change will come as a result of a process that may take at least a couple of months of consistently applying the techniques and skills as explained in this book.

Before You Continue

Even though this is a paper book, it is intentionally designed to be *interactive*. That's because my goal is to help you not just read this book but actually use it to your advantage. For this reason, you will find "signposts" along the way in this book that will lead you to a bonus section of this book.

The bonus section contains printables designed to help you start getting positive results even more quickly.

http://geni.us/fgmbonus

When you register for the first time you will receive your private permanent link to your bonus area with all the worksheets from the signposts you will come to as you read. And, you'll also be eligible to receive the goodies that I occasionally send only to my VIP readers.

How to Feel Good Using This Book

In this book, I'm going to ask you to do something that has become somewhat unfashionable in our society of instant fixes and solutions- I'm going to ask you to do some thinking! Then I'm going to ask you to do some homework.

These are short exercises, but please make sure you actually complete them. Don't just skip over them and tell yourself you'll do them another time. These exercises are amongst the most important parts of this book. Have a pen and paper handy.

Most of the exercises are designed for you to do by yourself. If some aren't, it's specifically outlined. Maybe your spouse isn't ready yet. That's more common than not. But don't worry. If an exercise requires both of you to cooperate, and you feel your spouse is not quite ready, leave it. Just continue practicing other exercises, and give your partner some more time. When you feel "safe" enough to do a particular exercise, do it together. You will see how fast things will begin to change.

Even though you might not agree on everything (and I encourage you to do so), I believe the principles explained in this book pass the test of common sense, and work in any relationship. But I do not claim my truth is the only truth. Instead of assuming that my suggestions are one size fits all, please realize that different couples will experience different benefits from this book. This is neither a shortcoming nor an apology. It's just the way it is.

I recommend using the book as reference material, reading it in the sequence it's written, trying things on your own, and then continuing.

Remember, even though some exercises may seem strange to you at first, after trying them a few times, you'll have a different impression, and that's when you'll begin to see some changes-in your thoughts and feelings, and then you'll be able to start getting different results.

In the book, sometimes I use the term partner and sometimes I use spouse, and I exchange the terms marriage and relationship. That said, I don't care whether you are married or not. I don't care if you are heterosexual or not. What I care about, and believe in, is that we are all equal in wanting to be happy, feel understood, accepted and loved, and that is what I am after here.

Once you've finished the book, make the commitment to take some immediate action and, most importantly, persist. There is no way around that. You've made an investment here, in both your time and money. It's quite shocking to think that there will be people who have purchased this book only to feel better, but who won't have even read this far! The fact that you're still here shows that you're an action taker. So don't let yourself down by not following through with some immediate action, and persisting.

There is more good news. If you follow this book, you will be able to see results fairly soon. You won't have to wait for months with no sign of any improvement. Still, the lasting change will come as a result of you consistently applying the techniques and skills as explained. That's where establishing good habits will help.

It might be a good idea to start writing a journal. If you haven't done it before, this is a good time to try it out. For the sake of the experience and the journey you are about to embark on with this book, start now. Even though it's not necessary, I encourage you to do this, because you WILL reap huge benefits.

Journaling will help you get to know yourself and your partner much better. Through journaling, you will become a better person. Furthermore, it will be a memory of your path toward the intimate marriage that you are striving for. You'll be able to revisit the ups and downs, look back and say, "Hey, we did it! We turned it around. Life is good."

Lastly, if your relationship is in trouble right now, it didn't get to this point over night. It grew to this point, and now it might be overwhelming, and you don't know where to start. But don't worry. Even if repairing your relationship looks to you like a giant elephant now, you know what they say about how to eat an elephant; one bite at a time. Well, go to the next chapter and take your first bite.

My Journey

I'd like to share my story because I believe many of you have what you consider to be a "normal" life, just as I thought I'd had. But you may not be sure if it's really how it's supposed to be.

My wife and I had a normal life. To many of our friends and outside observers, it seemed almost like a perfect life. Both of us had good jobs, we bought a house, we had a family, we frequently went on nice vacations and, on top of that, we were doing great financially.

Seven years after we were married, our second son was born. It's also the time I left the corporate world and started my own company. With the new baby, and me working on my new business, things started to get worse.

Together but Lonely

Fast forward a couple of years, and things were much worse.

I worked a lot, and came home late. The working days literally flashed by. After the kids had gone to bed, I would work even more, there in the living room with my laptop on my lap, quite often until early in the morning. My wife would be on the couch, mostly watching reality shows, only to fall asleep soon after, right there on the couch. When I finished working early in the morning, I would wake her up, and we both would go to bed. That was what my working week looked like. We'd spend weekends somewhere outside. I think that was my way of making it up to the kids and, at the same time, avoiding spending idle time together with my wife, because I feared yet another argument or criticism. We both did.

Then, after years of building my company, I didn't enjoy running it. It was an increasing source of stress for me, even though I was making good money. I simply didn't enjoy it anymore.

My wife was not happy and we were not happy, not as a couple nor as a family.

My wife would complain, and tell me that we had grown apart. I didn't believe her, and I told her she exaggerated. I was slowly getting fed up with constantly reminding her that she should think more positively about life. I honestly didn't feel that we were having any more or less troubles than the average couple. I guess I wanted to believe that.

Warning Signs

Looking back, I know now that my wife saw things quite accurately, much more accurately than I did. We weren't okay, but I was not aware of how bad a condition we were really in.

To illustrate what I mean, let's have a look at some of the traits of an imaginary couple who's relationship is in trouble. Their relationship can be described by:

- Lots of criticism, frequently disguised as sarcastic remarks.

- Blaming and pulling out events from the past.

- She's spending most of her evenings watching TV, while he spends most of his free time on a computer.

- Silent treatments.

- Both have stopped doing nice, little things for each other (you know, when you do something for your loved one just because, expecting nothing in return).

- They have almost no fun together, aside from occasional meetups with friends.

- She spends more time talking to her friends in a day then talking to him in a week.

- They rarely compliment each other.

- Honest praise or admiration is hard to find, if at all.

- She complains in an "All is on me" fashion, while he is feeling unappreciated for all the stuff that he is doing for the family.

- Both are quick to notice what doesn't work, and how the other has screwed up (again), but slow to notice the good stuff. What good stuff??

- They fight frequently, and the fights seem to come from nowhere.

- After the fight, one would initiate talking things through, but the other one avoids it, for fear of ending up in another exhaustive argument, yet again.

- As talking things through is so exhausting, less and less conversations about their relationship take place until there is none.

- Sex is infrequent, sometimes it's weeks before they might be intimate again.

The list reads like a user's manual of things NOT to do if you want to have a healthy relationship.

The problem is this list was my wife and me. It's an exact snapshot of my own marriage at the time when we were in the deepest trouble.

The Vicious Cycle

It wasn't bad all the time, though. We had normal periods as well. The normal periods were exchanged with the bad periods in almost predictable cycles. During the normal time, we were reasonably fine and things would kind of settle down. During those times, we would do what average couples do and more. We would hang out and regularly dedicate time to go out, typically having dinner, just the two of us, something we enjoyed then and still enjoy now. I think that alone, together with a big, fat deposit of good memories from the early days, helped save our butts. When things were normal, we would be intimate, though from today's point of view, I wouldn't say that we had a great sex life, but it was fine at the time. In short, during the normal periods, while things were not perfect, we were content. At least I was.

Of course, things were not right.

After a fight, I would usually initiate talking things through, but many times we would end up even more upset than before. Then, after a couple of days of the silent treatment, mostly initiated and perpetuated by myself, things would get better for a while. But only until the next remark or innocent action. Then it started all over again.

We both seemed to know what to say to set the other one off. We were masters at that. But, the scary thing was that the frequency and the duration of the bad times were increasing rapidly.

Things came to a point when we couldn't tell anymore what was normal and what wasn't. We'd gotten so used to constant tension, that it became a part of who we were and how we lived. This was killing us, but we didn't know what to do to stop the madness.

On my part, I mostly felt lonely. I didn't think that my wife supported me, or that she was truly my closest friend and ally, no matter what. She used to be my greatest cheerleader, but this was now gone. I felt resented and rejected. She wouldn't talk to me anymore, and I felt disgust from her when I was talking about my job. I'm a big boy, and I can take many things, but after exhausting days at my business, then coming home and getting the silent treatment, or hearing constant complaining and bitching about what a bad husband and father I was, this "all is on me" complaining, as if there was nothing I did for the family, took its toll. It's not that we were mean. My wife did indeed believe that I didn't care about her and the family. She resented me for that, and I surely felt it all too well. I also felt unappreciated for many things, including the chores and the work with the children that I did. She was completely blind to the good stuff.

I understand this now, but at the time I didn't, and it drove me nuts. As I'll discuss later, this is quite common. Negative perception of one's partner is a real killer of relationships, more so than lack of communication skills.

That said, it's easy to fall into such a vicious cycle, and hard to break out of if you don't know the right sequence of steps to take. My wife and I found the way to break the cycle, and this book will teach you how you can do it, too.

There's one other aspect to all this, as well. I was becoming increasingly tense, especially around the children. If tension could be sold, I could have earned a fortune, as I was producing it in vast quantities. Years later, I realized how disconnected I was with my children, even though I loved them more than anything.

The Toll on the Kids

All of this trouble had, of course, taken its toll on our kids. We weren't aware of it at the time, but looking back on it now, it was obvious. There were too many signs showing us exactly this, but we didn't want to admit it.

Our oldest son reacted to our problems by withdrawing, and not showing the pain he was obviously feeling. He was out of the more vulnerable early years so, in that sense, he was lucky. But it was our youngest son, Nik, who was hit the hardest by our marriage problems. At the time when our problems were at their peak, he was between the ages of two and five.

Nik holds a special place as savior in the healing of our marriage, because it was he who triggered the healing. How is that? During most of the years he was attending kindergarten, he was a disaster, filled with anger. From early on, he showed a passion for all sorts of weaponry that we couldn't explain. Guns, killings and death were topics he paid particular attention to. Aside from those, he wasn't interested in playing normal games like the other children did. He liked LEGO® bricks a lot, but only to make guns out of them. Then he would point the gun at himself, or aim and shoot at the other children. He was overly aggressive and, at times, dangerous to the other children. And he enjoyed hurting himself. His teacher reported that he would stand in front of the mirror and slap himself in the face. It almost seemed like there was some dark force within him that preoccupied him with negative thoughts, weapons, destruction, cutting, stabbing and all sorts of things not at all appropriate for a child of his age.

Although Nik was difficult at home, most of these things he did at kindergarten. Many times we weren't told of them, until one day when his teacher invited us for a talk. We had a long talk. It was sobering in a way. When we heard the details of all that was happening, we were thankful to Nik's teacher for her big heart, and frightened at the same time. If you've seen the movie *We Need To Talk About Kevin* you know what I mean. On advice from the teacher, we enrolled Nik in a program that offered help to children with behavior disorders. We spent almost two years going from one child counselor to another with him, visiting a number of different child specialists almost every other week. During those times, they did all sorts of evaluations on our son. Of course, he lacked some skills, but he was extremely good at others. The conclusion of the evaluations was that there was nothing wrong with the boy.

No wonder! It took us a full two years to slowly realize by ourselves that our son Nik wasn't the problem. It was us, my wife and I, who were the problem. It was us! The kindergarten teacher suspected that from the beginning, but couldn't tell us straight out. In all her wisdom, she knew that when the student is ready, the teacher will appear. And so it happened.

I didn't want to live the rest of my life like this. I thought I deserved better. I knew I had to change things radically as there wasn't any sense in repeating the same old patterns that led to the problems in the first place.

The following year, I sold my company to my business partner. The company that I had spent years building, and that had kept me away from my family. I decided to devote myself to my children and my marriage for as long as it took to get our peace and stability back. Consequently, it lead me to where I am now. I have never looked back.

Nowadays, Nik is worlds apart from where he was when things were bad. It's been such a dramatic change that, if I hadn't experienced it first hand, I would never have believed it. But it was our youngest son and his unbearable behavior that eventually made us realize that it was in fact our relationship that needed a major overhaul. If it wasn't for Nik, it might have been too late for us. We could have screwed up our marriage beyond repair.

And that nearly happened.

Almost Divorced at the Lasting Love Seminar

I can still remember everything as if it was yesterday. The funny thing is we were at a seminar on lasting love for couples when it happened. Thinking about it today, it almost feels like some kind of a bad joke.

Let me give you a bit of background.

Even though Nathaly and I had perpetual problems in our marriage, we had gotten so used to them that it never crossed our minds to seek professional help or, at least start reading some good books on the topic. I find that astonishing today, but at the time I thought, "Why should I? She's the one who has to change."

The problem was that we both felt like this. Both of us had a growing, negative perception of one another in our heads telling us that if the other would change, everything would be fine. I honestly believed that I wasn't making any significant mistakes in our marriage. I believed that if I could make my wife realize how wrong she was about us, everything would be just fine.

So, aside from countless and fruitless conversations followed by further arguing and anger, we didn't do much to educate ourselves.

It happened that my wife found a seminar on the Internet. The seminar, Lasting Love for Couples, promised to reveal "the secrets" to, well ... lasting love for couples. To tell you the truth, I didn't feel like going. I thought no one could give you a recipe for a better marriage in two days. And the name of the seminar was a bit cheesy for my taste as well.

But, out of consideration for my wife, I agreed to go. I thought, if it's important to her, than that's good enough for me. And, I thought we needed some time just for ourselves, and the fresh sea air couldn't hurt. I prepared myself mentally to go there with the best possible attitude.

The Ride

Things did not begin well. We started fighting on the ride to the seminar.

Logically thinking, even if you're driving to a seminar that teaches lasting love, it doesn't mean that you will magically drop the old, bad behavior patterns. We surely didn't. I mean, going to a seminar that taught how to achieve lasting love, while being mad at each other even before getting there, isn't such a great start. We drove the remaining distance in stone silence. It felt almost surreal, but that's how it was.

The seminar itself was a nice blend of interesting guest lecturers, speaking on marriage and relationships that got you thinking, accompanied by healthy food, Tai Chi and yoga classes, super healthy smoothies made from vegetables, and many other things that by this point I wasn't doing much of. So there we were at the sea coast in a nice hotel, surrounded by pine trees, smelling salty, fresh April breezes, and attending the Lasting Love for Couples seminar.

The Word Was Spoken

On the second day of the seminar, while we had our first break for lunch, my wife took a little nap, as she always did when she felt bad and unhappy, and I took a long walk, nurturing my own thoughts in my head as I always did. I walked along the coast for an hour, while having a great internal monologue. Boy, how smart I was in my head, full of marital wisdom, thinking and devising a strategy of how I was going to prove to my wife that the only thing she had to change was her overly negative perception of me, and then our marriage and everything else would be fine. I thought about the strategy, and how I was going to say this without upsetting her too much, while still getting the message across.

We had lunch later, and it was awkward. The two of us sat there, having nothing to say to each other. Even though we'd had disagreements before, this was still very unusual for us. We always had something to talk about, if nothing else, then about our jobs and children. I can remember watching other couples with nothing to say to each other during an entire meal, and how I pitied them. Now, we were that couple. Stone silence, each one with his and her own thoughts. But in my head, accusations were raging, things I wanted to say to her, but expected she either wouldn't listen or we'd end up in a fight again. I didn't want to do that in a restaurant, and certainly not at the seminar.

My wife then said something I will never forget. She said she was thinking that it would be for the best if we divorced. She said she wanted a divorce, and we could take care of children together.

So there we were. The word had been spoken, loud and clear.

This was a point I never believed I would get to. Sure, the word divorce had been said a couple of times before, but it always felt harmless, like she didn't really mean it.

Now it was different; she said it calmly. No crying, although tears began to come slowly. She said it with a surprising firmness, as if she'd thought everything through with a kind of determination. It felt like she was determined that this was the right thing to do, and she had reached her conclusion.

It seemed surreal to me. Feelings ranged from a disbelief that this was really happening, to anger. At that very moment, I was angry, not so much because of us, but because I thought about our two beautiful sons, and the suffering they would have to go through. It wasn't fair. I was thinking about the disappointment of my parents. I was thinking about what our friends will say. All sorts of stuff.

My ego was even angrier. It seemed outrageous to me for my wife to even propose something like that. To me! To me, who is doing everything to make this marriage work!

Well, she did, and there was nothing I could do to unsay the words that had just been said.

There was silence for ten seconds or so, then I heard myself saying, "Fine. I don't think this is a solution, and I think we'll both be very sorry if we do this. But if that's what you really want, then go and find where the grass is greener." I couldn't help saying it with a patronizing tone that probably pissed her off instantly, and reminded her that she'd made the right decision.

Fighting Back the Ego

We stood in silence while I paid the bill, then headed back to the seminar room where the afternoon courses were about to begin. While we were walking, I thought to myself, "Wait a second. What a joke! I am here walking toward a seminar to learn how to achieve lasting love with someone who doesn't want me anymore! Hell no! I'll just go to the bar and have a drink. Screw the seminar." So, she went upstairs alone, and I headed toward the bar. My head was buzzing, because this time it was different. This wasn't the usual stuff.

As I was ordering my drink, it hit me; thoughts of the good times came to mind, and us having good times with the kids. Even though my ego was offering heavy opposition, my inner voice was saying, "Do you really want to let it go so easily? Go up and talk to her." This wasn't a game anymore. This was it. My life, our life. I turned around and went upstairs.

I entered the seminar room where the next module of the seminar was beginning. I sat down away from my wife, because I didn't feel like being next to her. I can't honestly remember what they were talking about at the course during this hour. My head was buzzing, as I still didn't want to believe this was really happening. To me!

When a break came, I went to my wife and touched her gently on her shoulder and said, "Please come with me. I have something to tell you. Let's go to our room." I was afraid she wouldn't want to. But she didn't turn me down.

The Reunion

We went to our hotel room, and spent the whole afternoon talking. Obviously, something radical had to happen in order for the two of us to be ready to finally start listening to each other, for the first time in many years. We were both facing the real possibility (not just empty threats) of a divorce that would seriously change our lives, no matter who was right or who was wrong.

It helped that we truly did love each other deeply. We had a rich history of doing things together and spending time together as a couple. I guess we banked on those memories. Banking on memories of the good times saved us. Today I can write about it, but back then it was a lucky coincidence. I believe that creating good memories with one another is one of the most critically important pillars of any successful relationship. We'll talk about that later in this book.

We talked and we cried. We told each other how we really felt, and the reasons that lead to the way we reacted to some of the most intensive fights we could remember. We explained to each other the past, and some of the frustrations from our childhoods. It took a full afternoon and half the evening, and we never returned to the seminar that day. The other participants went to dinner together, and we went to a nice dinner alone, and talked some more.

It was like we finally managed to crack a big, heavy lock on the door to our connection. That was the evening that we would once again feel each other after such a long time, and finally be heard and listened to. To an extent, we both got insight and perspective on the events that had bothered us in the past. What a relief this was, I cannot even tell you.

Reality Check

Even though we enjoyed the rest of the weekend at the seminar, feeling much more connected and temporarily happy, we both knew something. The next time one of us stepped on the other's toes it will probably be the same old story again. You know when things come out of nowhere, and the next thing you know, you're fighting again?

At the time, we thought it was the fighting that was our major problem. In a way it was, but that was only the symptom of something much deeper. We both knew, right at the conclusion, that we had to seek help with it.

We were realistic enough to admit to each other that, even though we loved one another, this was killing our relationship. Both of us, each in our own ways, were afraid that if we continued to do things in the same manner as we had been (that obviously didn't work), the day will come where there will simply not be any energy left to save our marriage.

The Cease Fire

We decided to get professional help. We agreed that we would search for a good marriage counselor. We didn't have a clue who we should go to, so we checked online, did some further research, visited and talked with some of them, and finally selected a couple's counselor who we both felt fine with.

Only that she wasn't available. She was about to leave the country, and the earliest we could meet was in a couple of months, as she wasn't working over the summer. After talking to her over the phone, we had a good feeling about her so we decided to wait.

We also agreed that, until we got some professional help, we would restrain from all negativities as much as possible.

You could call this a cease fire. Even though we both knew that it was not a permanent solution, we felt we needed some peace, even an artificial one. After all, after our long talk, and the beautiful days of the weekend at the Eternal Love seminar behind us, we felt we could survive the additional couple of months without further scratches.

I'd asked the counselor, until we met with her, if she could recommend any books so we could educate ourselves before hand.

She did. In fact she sent a whole array of titles. We started to read them, and the process began.

The Process

That's how it all started. I was swallowing literature. I traveled and learned, and compared the learnings to what we were doing at home. And, in this book is everything I learned through it all.

I'd realized that there were reasons why we had been behaving as we were. I'd realized that my wife is not crazy, and that I am not hallucinating. I got familiar with a number of different theories, techniques and skills that promised to help couples overcome their troubles. Some proved to be very helpful, some were okay, some not at all.

The more I studied, the more I got hooked. The more I started to understand the nature and dynamics of intimate relationships, the more I got interested. The more I understood about relationships, the more I realized how very wrong I was about certain things in our marriage, and how right I was in believing that we could make it work.

As I was lucky enough to have my wife with me on this journey, it was a journey of two from the beginning, and we tested everything that this book covers. Many things didn't quite work, and we messed up many times in the process, but eventually we got it right, and this book is going to reveal to you our findings.

Results Today

We now feel more connected than ever before. We feel each other even when no words are spoken. We laugh and have fun frequently. Most of all, we are looking forward to spending time with each other. We are looking forward to doing the little, nice things for each other. We get along with our children. The problems have vanished.

We know and understand each other's wounds from the past. Being aware of them makes it easier to forgive and move on.

Sex is great, and I can't understand how I thought it just was fine before. In short, life is good.

But it's not all just bliss.

I wish I could tell you that, but it's really not so. We have disagreements, and on occasions we fight. As a matter of fact, we had a fight the night before I wrote this. We still mess up, and we behave not exactly in line with the teachings of this book. But you know what? We just say, tomorrow we'll do better, learn from it, and get back to practicing what we've learned, and we are just fine. That is a big difference from what was happening years back, and it gives us great confidence in our relationship.

Let me tell you, though. It wasn't achieved overnight. It took us years to figure it out. You are now in a much better position by having this book because you have a short cut.

My mission is to let you know how I achieved these results so you can try them on your own. Knowing what I know now, I am 100 percent sure you can make your relationship better. There is nothing mystical about it, but the results are magical.

And the last thing, don't trust me. Trust your own experiences. The issue of trust is one big hokum anyway. All we hear is a constant trust me, trust me, trust me. Why the hell should you trust me? We don't know each other. That's why I take a different stance: there is no reason to believe in an approach until *after* it works. If it doesn't work, then there is no reason to believe in it. So, contrary to many of the books that build an author's immense, professional credibility, as well as professional titles as your trusted guide, don't trust me. Trusting me will not make your relationship any better. Trusting yourself, on the other hand, will.

Things No One Told Us When We Got Married

I don't pretend that I've cracked the code to a healthy and long lasting relationship. Human relationships are way too complex for anyone to claim something like that. That said, by studying relationships, talking to couples who have made it, and observing what I do right and wrong in my own marriage, I have found common elements of that puzzle called a rock solid, feel-good marriage.

The Blueprint to a Feel Good Marriage

I believe any change, including repairing your relationship, starts where it should-in your head. It starts with your thoughts, and ends with creating habits that you learn in order to support getting what you want and sustaining it. In that sense it is a plan and I've named it the *Seven Step Feel Good Marriage Plan.*

A benefit to the *Feel Good Marriage Plan* is it allows baby steps. Baby steps make it much more likely for you to achieve progress, because the process doesn't demand that you transform yourself into the perfect David and Victoria Beckham.

The steps:

1. Start your *feel good* marriage in your head. Apply the right mindset. Have realistic expectations, and an accurate perception of your marriage and your partner. Know what you want. Set and maintain high standards for your relationship.

2. Reconnect and be friends (again) by creating a loving and *feel good* atmosphere every day.

3. Shut up and listen *good*. Then, know how to say things mindfully so you can talk each other into *feeling good*.

4. Learn how to turn minor disagreements into *feel good*, no-big-deal conflicts, so they become connection points instead of causing yet another blow to your relationship.

5. Learn how to make piece with the past and reconnect with your spouse on a much deeper level. In another words, get over it and get on with *feeling good*.

6. Peek into your *feel good* future together and develop a shared vision of your relationship.

7. Set up habits and rituals to make your new *feel good* behaviors stick.

Everything that happens between your thoughts (No. 1) and your habits (No. 7) is a set of specific skills and behaviors. As I believe successful relationships are acts of doing and not having, I believe all of these steps can be taught.

Think of it like a craftsman's tool chest, only it's loaded with tools that a couple needs to get their relationship in good shape, and to keep it there. Some tools are needed more frequently, and some a bit less, but all of them are essential.

If you were a maintenance person responsible for your house, in the top drawers of your tool chest, you'd probably have tools like screwdrivers, pliers, maybe your favorite two hammers, and a couple of adjustable wrenches. They would be there, right at eye level. They're the tools that are used most often. In fact, you'd probably have them in your leather tool belt so they'd be readily available. These would be the things you do to reconnect with your partner on a daily basis, your listening skills and saying things mindfully, as well as managing disagreements.

Then, you would have the tools you use less frequently in the middle drawers. Those would be things like a wrench and some socket sets, crowbar, and everything related to working with electricity. They would all be right there in the middle. They might not be needed on an every day basis, but when they are, they are irreplaceable. In your relationship these would be the skills to overcome stuff that is bigger than everyday disagreements, the stuff that can seriously damage your relationship.

Then there are the bottom drawers. These contain the least used tools, like plumbing supplies. While these are rarely used, they are invaluable when some plumbing work is required. This would be your skill of creating, and then occasionally revisiting, your vision of your relationship.

Most of what I'd found out there concentrated on teaching only one or two aspects of the puzzle, such as how to communicate (No. 3), and how to manage disagreements and conflicts (No. 4). But little was published that provided a balanced view on all of the pieces, and in the right sequence, ready to be implemented right away. The right sequence makes things easier.

I have intentionally left a great sex life off the list of the Seven Step Feel Good Marriage Plan, because I believe great sex is a consequence of the good behaviors in the plan.

By following the seven steps, which will be explained in greater detail later, you will naturally boost your sexual desire. And, more importantly, because you'll be able to change the very metabolism of your relationship, and install good habits, you will continue to enjoy the benefits of a higher sexual desire for years to come.

Setting the Stage

Before we move on let me tackle a couple of things that many people aren't aware of:

Your thoughts determine what you get

It is where it all starts-with your thoughts. It's the thoughts that make us feel good or bad about something, and it's our feelings that determine how we will behave. It's our behavior that determines what results will we have. And it's our constant behavior in certain ways that creates habits, which in the long run, determine who we really are and what we stand for.

Therefore, right at the beginning, this book starts with a little bit of brain work. Don't worry, we won't be covering human anatomy or anything close to that. We will be covering some basics about your brain that will help you to understand why your partner behaves as they do, and why you behave as you do.

The almighty communication myth

If I ask people with relationship problems what they think they should change first to improve their relationships, most of them would say they should improve their communication skills.

That's exactly the problem. Most of the books and seminars I've seen out there, as well as in traditional counseling, are almost obsessive about communication.

Sure, you need to have skills to know how to listen carefully and say something mindfully. We'll talk about that. Then again, if you and your partner almost hate each other, are you really prepared to communicate nicely? You have to feel safe and understood first, and it's only then will you have a chance to be heard, and only then can you start to really listen.

Change the energy of your relationship

In line with what I said above, getting better at communication skills is necessary, but it's not enough. It's one element of the whole puzzle, and a not so important one.

To achieve long term results, you have to change the very "energy" of your relationship, the metabolism of the relationship.

Metabolism is how well and how fast you can convert the food and drink you put inside your body into energy that keeps you going. Most important, your metabolism also determines your long-term chances of achieving and sustaining your ideal weight. If you are overweight (or underweight) I bet your metabolism isn't quite right.

Similarly, it's your relationship's metabolism that determines how healthy and long-lasting your relationship will be. To change your relationship's metabolism, you have do the right things in the right order.

The recipe for being permanently unhappy

Expectations are by definition constructs in our head. We construct an idea of what something should look like, how it should feel and sound, and every other imaginable attribute we can think of. Then we compare what's in our head to reality.

The problems come if those expectations are false in their foundations, or if they're outright unrealistic. Why? Because it's the perfect recipe for being permanently unhappy. Not only is it a perfect recipe for feeling bad permanently, but it's also a very effective way to drive other people away, namely-your partner or spouse. This book covers several of the most common aspects of false expectations, which leads us to the next point.

All you need is love

It's what the Beatles sing. Love will do the magic. This is a big myth. Sure, successful couples love each other deeply, but they don't rely on loving feelings to come naturally. They create them. Love is not an act of having, but an act of doing.

By using a system of skills and specific behaviors and habits, those couples create and foster a loving atmosphere every single day.

I repeat, every single day, and not only for their anniversary or during vacations.

That said, I'm not saying that falling in love is a system. To love or to be in love are two completely different things. Falling and being in love is just a temporary stage in a relationship where no system can ever win.

You probably have never thought about it this way, but being in love is like being on drugs, only that our very own brains are producing those drugs. No wonder people say being in love is being crazy. It's a special time for anyone to experience, and it should stay so.

Expecting your early romance days to last forever

Expecting the early romance days to last forever is a great and very common example of a false expectation. Many couples actually divorce because one of them, or perhaps both, realize that the feelings they had in their early romance days are gone. Then they figure it must be because they don't love each other anymore. What a mistake!

Later in the book I'll explain what exactly is happening in the three distinctive stages of a relationship. My goal is to equip you with the tools that will help you get to the third stage of the relationship that we call the real love. Stay tuned!

The grass is greener myth

Too many couples divorce believing that things will be completely different with another person. But somehow they end up in a relationship with exactly the same kind of a person that they'd divorced only some time ago. Almost everything remains the same except for the person they are with.

As people realize that their partner is not the same person who they were during the courtship period, they feel betrayed and confused. The darker side of the partner they tend to point a finger to shows up.

Couples have a hard time grasping the fact that they live with another person, so they start "changing" that person to fit their idealized image of the perfect partner. People are funny. When something doesn't work, they try the same thing, even harder!

Eventually, as they realize that changing their partner doesn't work, they figure that it's just bad luck, and they married the wrong person this time. They insist on that idealized picture in their head, and they keep searching. This is another flavor of the above mentioned recipe for being permanently unhappy.

Successful couples have learned to resist the grass is greener myth-in other words, someone else will make me happy. They have learned to put their energy into making themselves and their marriage better. They have learned to love the strengths of each other, but they have also learned to love the weaknesses, as well. They begin solving problems by asking themselves, "What can I do to change things." Instead of, as too many do, thinking that they are married to the wrong person.

Your past determines your future

Wrong. Your past does NOT determine your future.

You might be discouraged by failed attempts to repair your relationship. You might be tempted to believe that your partner will never change. Many people generalize experiences they've had in the past and project them into the future. We all do that from time to time.

But the fact is that your future together hasn't been written yet. Your relationship is full of opportunities, and opportunities lie ahead, in the future.

> *The best thing about the past is that it's over.*
> *The best thing about the future is that it's yet to come.*
> *The best thing about the present is that it's here.*
>
> —*Dr. Richard Bandler*

Just because you've been fighting with your partner all the time, doesn't mean that it will stay that way forever. But it does mean you should learn to try some new things as, obviously, the stuff that you've been doing up until now hasn't worked so well. And, by the way, this is exactly what you're doing right now, you are learning something new.

Imagine what life would be like if the future was only a repetition of past experiences. What a sad, sad world that would be. Not to mention the fact that by doing so, we would still be living in caves, and eating raw meat and bitter roots.

I believe everyone can repair their relationship. Don't let anyone, even your own negative voice in your head, convince you otherwise.

Your Feel Good Marriage Starts In Your Head

Reading this book, I expect you to know that if you're doing something, and it's not working (and it's probably not if you're reading this book), there's got to be an easier way. And if what you are doing isn't working, then you've got to do something else.

Wise couples have learned that you have to approach problems differently to get different results. Often, minor changes in approach, attitude and actions make the biggest difference, and it's what I found out in my own marriage to be true.

Therefore, the first thing you've got to do is change your own mindset, because it's where everything starts. It's your mindset that can ruin or save your marriage.

Your Mindset

How couples think, and what partners believe about each other, affects how they perceive the other. Your mindset and attitude does matter. Changing behavior is important, but so is changing your mindset and attitude. Bad attitude leads to bad thoughts and bad feelings, which lead to bad results. On the other hand, positive attitude leads to positive thoughts, which lead to good feelings and positive behaviors. Positive behaviors become habits, and habits become part of who you truly are. That is how any change really happens.

If you are stuck in your relationship right now, chances are you feel frustrated and angry. If that's so, your spouse, and all the people around you, will pick up on that, and you'll just get more stuck.

If you are not happy, don't expect those around you to make you happy. They can't; it's not their job.

It's not the responsibility of your spouse or partner to make you happy. They can contribute to it, but ultimately this is a state that you have to manage yourself. You can't have happiness; you either are in a state of being happy or not.

But here is good news. You can influence this state by applying the right thoughts. And that can be learned. That's why the mindset is the first part of this book and that's why your mindset can be your best friend or worst enemy. Your mindset is absolutely essential if you really mean to repair your marriage, or make it even better than it is now.

You might say to yourself, how the hell I am supposed to be happy if we fight all the time? Worry not. One part of this book is dedicated to ways of dealing with anger constructively, even when your heart starts pumping like crazy, your face starts getting red and you would rather grab a gun than talk. That said, the skill of constructively expressing disagreement is a necessary skill, yet not sufficient enough to achieve a long lasting and healthy relationship.

For now, just note this: Here, it's about you. You took the initiative and you are now reading this book. So, forget about your spouse for a while, and just accept that we will talk and think about you for a large part of this book.

If you are reading this together, that is also valid, as both of you are individuals first, and a spouse to each other second. Changing your mindset means you are willing to start changing how you think about yourself, your partner and your relationship, how you feel, and eventually, how you behave and what you do every single day.

That is the right way to do things if you want a lasting change, and not just temporary good feelings like the ones you had because you went on vacation without the kids to an exotic island for a week.

Let's go through a couple of elements of the over-reaching mindset that you will start employing as you read this book. They are essential for you and your relationship to move forward, to repair it or to make it much better than it already is.

A Quick Tour Through Your Brain

Before we move on, I'd like you to take a moment and think about your brain. It's where your thoughts begin, and your beliefs are formed. It's where everything starts.

We already know that it's our thoughts that influence how we feel, and it's our feelings that influence how we are going to behave. And it's our behavior that influences the results we get out of life.

Knowing that, it's good to understand a couple of things about your brain, especially how the unconscious and conscious parts of your brain work together. It's namely our unconscious mind that interferes in our social interactions much more than we are aware of. As you will find out later, this becomes extremely important when trying to manage conflicts.

Let's do a really quick tour through our brains. It will be overly simplified because neither myself nor you is a brain surgeon, not that we need to be for the purposes of this book.

Our brains have evolved in three distinct phases, which is the brain stem, the limbic system and the cortex.

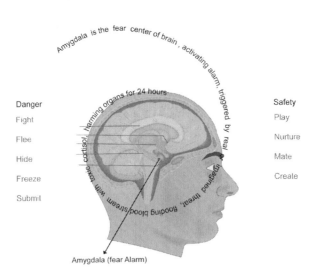

Amygdala (fear Alarm)

The brain stem controls signals sent from the brain to the body, which controls life supporting autonomic functions like breathing, blood pressure, and digestion.

Then there is the limbic system. One part of the limbic system is called the amygdala. It's a tiny, almond-shaped region of our brains, and very powerful. Among things such as pleasure from sex or eating, the amygdala is responsible for processing emotions, such as anger, fear and danger. When the amygdala perceives that you are in danger, it triggers a response automatically, and that can be fight, flee, hide, freeze or submit. Both the brain stem and limbic system are the oldest parts of the brain, and as such form our unconscious mind. You can call it "ancient brain" because it evolved first.

The cerebral cortex was the last to evolve. It's a complex and human part of the brain, associated with our conscious mind. This is the thinking part of the brain, in which we have the most control. It's responsible for reasonable thinking, judgments, conclusions, making decisions, and projecting things into the future.

Fun Facts About Your Brain

The celebral cortex may be complex and big, but has little power compared to the two older systems.

How so? Here are some facts about the amygdala, our "ancient brain."

- If the amygdala and our conscious mind (the cerebral cortex) were racing, the amygdala would already be at the finish line while the cerebral cortex would have just started the engine (started consciously thinking). That came quite handy in the early days of mankind. Imagine a beast coming toward the entrance of an ancient man's cave. It was simply a matter of survival to be able to respond quickly, whether it was fight, flight or hide.

- If your partner is yelling at you right now, your amygdala would treat this the same way as if the beast was trying to get into your cave, and eat you alive a thousand years ago. That's because the amygdala can't tell the time.

- If your partner gives you a sarcastic remark, it can evoke as strong a reaction as a life-threatening assault of a black bear chasing you in the woods. It's because the amygdala cannot tell the difference between symbolic danger (your thoughts triggered by a sarcastic remark) and literal danger (the bear chasing you). The cerebral cortex does know the difference though, but the amygdala is quicker.

- The amygdala doesn't remember names and faces. It cannot tell the difference between your mom shouting and calling you by your full name (which usually meant trouble, didn't it?), and your spouse doing the same many years later, but just wanting to talk to you.

- The amygdala is poisoning your organs each time it's activated by a real or imaginary threat. When this happens, it floods your blood stream with cortisol, harming your organs for 24 hours. That is why people who are happy and content with their lives have lower levels of cortisol, get sick less and live longer than unhappy people. Think of that next time you want to fight.

- Lastly, once the amygdala goes off, the cerebral cortex (conscious mind) shuts down and acts as if the brain needs to reboot before it can think clearly again. When anger settles, we often see things in a different perspective. Many times we are sorry for the words we said and things we did. Why? Because after a "reboot" our conscious mind is back in the game, and we behave "reasonably" again. Too many times the harm was done, and if we do it often enough it goes beyond repair. Think of that too. I'm mentioning this because, as a side effect of implementing this book in your life, you will improve your ability to prevent your conscious mind from completely shutting down, saving you many troubles in your relationship.

The Poor Me Syndrome

The "poor me" syndrome is common in relationships where couples refuse to grow as individuals, and, consequently, their relationship doesn't grow.

What do I mean?

In practice, this means that the ones who constantly complain about their partners have to be able to answer a simple question: "How have I contributed to this mess myself?" It's simple, yet so hard to so many. Those people are exactly the ones who don't feel happy in their relationships. Read that last sentence again.

But make no mistake. This doesn't mean that I suggest you become a martyr, and take it all on yourself. As we know, martyrs always die, that's why they are called martyrs. I don't want your relationship to die. What I do want is for you to stop thinking from a poor me victim perspective. Instead I want you to check, as honestly as you can, what you have done wrong and, even more important, what you have to do to put things where you want them to be.

Which leads me to the next question. Where do you want things to be? What do you want from your relationship anyway? It's crucially important to answer that question yourself, and I will help you do that a bit later.

Know this: people who constantly blame others, and complain about unhappy circumstances in their lives, become stuck in their role as a victim. Such a partner will never be able to grow and will, in fact, block the growth of their relationship.

And we don't want that, do we? So let's move on.

"But she drives me so crazy, when ..." "I just can't help it when he ..." Hearing that one, you can't help but think, "Who is in charge here, really?"

Who drives the bus?

We will learn here how to start thinking differently, and change your responses. And you can only do that by changing your thoughts, feelings and actions. You will learn how not to let your ancient brain part called the amygdala take over the steering wheel of your bus-your relationship and your life. You will learn how to live in a conscious relationship.

Update Your Expectations
to Feel Good

The goal of this section is to help you to get rid of some especially misleading beliefs and myths that cause unrealistic expectations in your relationship.

It's namely unmet expectations that make the perfect recipe for feeling permanently unhappy and stuck in your relationship, and life in general.

Throw Your Love Letters Away

Expecting romantic feelings to last forever is like expecting to win the lottery every time you play, no matter what the odds.

This expectation is being perpetuated by the mass media so much that it isn't a surprise that it's so common among couples, especially young ones.

The first moments of being in love are indeed passionate, intensive, without limitations and, in their own way, irrational, because they are so beautiful and unique. During that special time, we are flushed by ecstatic emotions that prevail over anything else, including common sense. We will soon find out why.

Let's walk through the three most distinctive stages of any relationship.

Stage One - Admiring yourself while on drugs

Why is being in love so intense and at times irrational?

Well, if you have been in love at least once, you'll surely remember. It was a special time when you could only see how beautiful she was, how smart he was, how everything she said was interesting, how much you loved the way he teased you about your cooking. This is the time when a newly found mate can't do or say anything wrong. And I am not being sarcastic here.

It's a scientifically proven fact that, during this time, our brains produce drugs that would be illegal on the street or need a medical prescription. To make us fall in love, our brains produce drugs like phenylethylamine (PEA), oxytocin, cortisol, dopamine, endorphins and hormones in massive quantities. This is why we say that people in love do not act reasonably. Who would?

So, what is actually happening during the time when we are in love?

The beautiful you

Personally, I agree with Mauricio Abadi and his definition of being in love: When we fall in love, we don't see our partner as he or she really is. Instead, the person of our desire serves as a screen onto which we project an idealized image of our ideal partner.

Abadi goes even further by saying that the image is actually your idealized image of yourself, being projected onto your newly found love. The person you are in love with is actually you, as you secretly want to be. It's like we take advantage of our new love as an object, just to be able to project, and then to look and admire our idealistic image of ourselves. We like the person we are in love with because they are kind enough to hold that mirror in front of us so adoringly, so that we can look at ourselves and enjoy being so perfect; everything we ever wanted to be. When in love, we are actually in love with an idealized picture of ourselves, projected onto another person.

So, we could say, it's kind of a fraud then, isn't it? Well, it actually is, only that both are playing along. The game goes on because we all want to be admired and loved so much that it really doesn't bother us that we are being taken advantage of. Even though deep down inside, we know we are not as ideal as our newly found mate thinks we are, but we play along, letting our mate do more of the same, holding the mirror with our idealized imagine even more so. Because it just feels so good to be admired with no reservation, who wants to spoil that? Yet the game we play is not really focused on our mate. It's a selfish game, as we enjoy looking at our idealized image more than caring who the person standing in front of us is. This doesn't sound romantic at all and it's not. Then again, neither are the misconceptions that happen as a result of such expectations, that the loving feelings are supposed to last forever, and if they don't, then we obviously haven't found the right partner. What a mistake!

This misperception is the source of many troubles in relationships, and that's not romantic either.

Maybe we should throw away those love letters in which our mate devotes his heart without reservation, and claims eternal love, telling us how perfect we are, because the receiver of those letters is not the right one. Your mate should address the letter to himself, instead.

But who does that in reality? No one. We all enjoy the feeling of being admired and loved. Therefore, being in love is not something that has even the slightest chance to survive for more than a limited amount of time.

Mother Nature made sure it's like that, as it simply isn't sustainable. It limits the in-love stage from a couple of weeks to a couple of months, with the exception of the celebrities who marry in Las Vegas. Those end in days.

Now, I understand you might not agree with this, and that's fine. Yet, it's a scientific fact that during that time, we are being fed massive amounts of drugs by our own brains that seriously damage our ability to think reasonably, and alter our perception of things, including of partner and ourselves.

Knowing this, it becomes easier to stop fantasizing about "the days when we first met," and dreaming of getting those feelings back. Just leave them where they belong; a nice memory that makes you smile.

But don't despair. This does not mean we're doomed to be unhappy in a relationship after the being-in-love phase inevitably ends. It's possible, and I will show you how. Yet, there is one step in between that proves to be the most challenging for most couples. Approximately half of couples manage to overcome it, leaving so many who don't.

Stage Two - The reality

This is the phase when you start seeing things differently. You start noticing things in your partner that you hadn't before. Actually, your eyes probably did see all of them, but your mind didn't. But if it did, you most likely found an appropriate explanation that fit your idealized picture of your mate. But inevitably, the power of the magic mirror starts to fade away. Things start to bother you. His jokes aren't so funny after all, her cooking is awful, you can't stand the way he leaves his clothes on the floor, and the sound of her laugh really gets on your nerves.

The "aha" moment

Even though just a few weeks before, you could not imagine he'd do something wrong, now you start noticing things, and it really annoys you. Our mate, after all, has flaws! Maybe, after all, they're not the princess or the prince that you'd thought they were! And, another interesting thing happens. Behavior that used to attract you to your mate in the first place (he is so relaxed) starts to bother you now (he is so lazy).

Changing your mate

When this "aha" moment starts to kick in, you have two choices: Either you stick to the picture of your idealized partner you hold in your head, and start changing him to fit to it, or you choose to love the man or woman in front of you as they are, and celebrate their strengths, and learn to love their weaknesses, just as much.

In another words, you either choose to stick to a construct in your head, or enjoy each other as you are, and go on from there, doing the beautiful things in life together.

Yet, many people choose to hold on to that picture in their heads. They choose to stick to their idealized image, trying to fit their partner into this artificial picture. Of course, many things will not fit. Some of them never will, so they'll start hating those parts of their partner. With time, the things that do not fit into the picture will take on more and more importance, while the majority of the good things in their relationship will start getting overlooked. It seems that after years, there won't be something that a spouse does or says that the other one will not perceive as negative, even if it was done or said with all the best intentions. It's like your partner is on a mission to prove she is right and you are wrong. In a way you are, because you don't fit to the idealized model, of which, most probably, you are not even aware.

When changing fails

So, in contrast to the things that happened when you were first in love, the projecting goes in the opposite direction. Only this time it has the potential to be deadly to your relationship. Before, nothing you did could be bad, now it seems like everything you do is perceived as such. Specific events are being generalized and overblown in their meaning, typically projected onto your mate's whole personality. Your partner gets criticized for who they are. It's not important who started it, because it's a vicious cycle; it feeds itself with the behavior of you both, albeit in different areas of your life together. Sadly, this vicious cycle, with time, only spins faster and faster. In many cases, it goes too far and people divorce. Or something worse happens. People choose to accept this as a fact of life, some kind of a law of nature, hating each other by inflicting wounds over and over again, and feeling miserable for not being accepted for who they are, loved unconditionally, respected and understood.

As said, many times people seek resolution in divorce, unaware that divorce is a permanent solution to a temporary problem. After they divorce, they discover that the same pattern starts repeating itself. Nothing has changed, only the person is different. Some issues may have a different twist, but at its core, the same issues will resurface. Five to ten years down the line, many people will regret this move. Well, it's usually only in the movies that things will get back to normal, but the reality is ... it's gone.

On the other hand, very few people regret that they decided to work on their marriage. Working on it doesn't mean you keep telling your partner he is horrible, or telling yourself you've tried everything. It's using the techniques in this book, along with other valuable resources, and then persisting until it works.

Stage Three – The real love

There are couples who manage to enter into a third stage of their relationship. They know how to reject the projections and start accepting their mate as he or she really is, with all their strengths and weaknesses. Remember we talked about constructing stuff in your head, or getting the most of what is available and learning to love the things you don't like? Well, this is it. This is what true love is all about. It's when you are no longer your main focus, but your spouse is. When you truly care how your spouse feels. When you love your partner just the way he is, and not the way your idealized image is telling you he should be.

It's a state where you enjoy being around each other so much that any particular disagreement is not another blow to your relationship, but just another opportunity to grow together. By solving your issues, you'll feel even more connected. It's when the good feelings and the joy of being around each other start to become more important than anything else. Then it starts to be fun, enjoyable and fulfilling to be around someone who is genuinely interested in what is happening to you, and how you are feeling, who genuinely wants to know what you need, and who enjoys helping you get it, for their own pleasure. Reread those last four words. For their own pleasure. Not because he expects to get a favor back, but because he loves you and would do it even though you may never return the favor.

Summary

- We are in love with similarities, but we love differences.
- Being in love means being in love with an idealized image of yourself in your head. To love means loving your partner's strengths and weaknesses, and accepting them as they are.
- The first stage of a relationship is romantic love. It's when you want the other person.
- The second stage is the power struggle when you want the other person to satisfy you.
- The third stage is "real love", and it's when you want what is best for the other person.

Seeking the Perfect Spouse

You can create constructs in your head, and seek the perfect someone for your whole life, but this will only make you permanently unhappy. On the other hand, you can search for what's available out there, and make the best of it. I'm not saying that you should marry anyone on the street and then make the best out of it, but that you should enjoy the qualities of your partner that you love and admire, and accept those that you don't while learning to love them just as much. The person you fell in love with, you fell in love for a reason. And from there on, you have to accept that your partner is not perfect and will never be. Same as you.

It's not about finding the right person,
but being the right person.

So the sooner we stop dreaming about having a perfect partner, dreaming about having a fairy-tale relationship with no conflicts, and having eternal loving feelings, the better.

Life gets considerably better when we decide that we will enjoy what we have instead of torturing ourselves because our dreams and fantasies didn't materialize.

So, are you with the perfect partner? Nope. Because no such partner exists. But you probably already have a perfect partner for YOU; it's just that your partner hasn't developed his or her full potential yet. And this is where you come in, with what you are doing right now.

Stop Changing Your Partner and Start Changing Yourself

When relationship troubles start, we tend to point a finger in another direction, mainly at our spouse. We know to the last detail what our partner will have to do or change in order to get our relationship back on track again.

Some of you might wonder, "Why should I change (first)? It's him (her) that has to change, and everything will be fine!"

I often hear things like:

- If only he would listen.

- If only she would understand me.

- I've tried everything and I don't know what to do anymore. (I've tried to change her, but it doesn't work.)

- If only he wouldn't come home so late. (Everything would be fine.)

- If only he would do more housework, everything would be great. (And all my problems would vanish.)

- If only she wouldn't nag all the time. (Our life would be perfect.)

- If only she wouldn't be so negative all the time. (We'd be great.)

- If only (insert your own favorite complaint).

Right.

Except that, such thinking will lead you nowhere. Probably, your partner expects and thinks the same, just on another area of your life. So, you both wait for each other to change. And no one does because you both think the other has to change. Which means you are stuck. Does this sound like a good plan to you? I know this because I was there for too many years. We'll tackle the consequences of this a little bit later.

Couples spend an unbelievable amount of energy trying to prove they're right, and that in fact it's their partner who is wrong. This is an attitude that doesn't help. Many have a hard time accepting the fact that they probably have contributed to their relationship troubles themselves.

If you are experiencing problems in your relationship right now, odds are that this attitude alone has led you to the exact situation you are in. And, if it hasn't worked by now, why should it all of a sudden start working? This is why it's you who should change.

What you also need to understand is that, while you don't have absolute control what others do and say to you, you do have a choice when it comes to how you react to it. Things can and will happen to you. Things will be said to you, sometimes with the intention to hurt you. Ultimately, your reaction will determine how this is going to affect your day.

No matter how hard you wish it to be so, you can't make yourself taller. It's impossible and futile.

It simply doesn't work. If it did, then you probably wouldn't be reading this book in the first place.

By the same token, let me ask you this: Do you really want to wait for your partner to change first so you can "prove" you are right? What happens then? How much time are you prepared to wait? What happens if you wait too long? What happens when you win (and your spouse loses)? Satisfaction? About what? Is there a prize you are expecting?

If you go down this path in your quest to change your partner and prove you're right, you may eventually end up being right and ... alone.

Yes, you may want to reread that last sentence. By the time you "prove" to your partner that you are right (according to your map of the world, of course), you might as well be filing papers for divorce.

So, let me ask you again: Do you want to wait for your partner to change, and prove you were right, and risk ending up alone, or are you prepared to look in the mirror and ask yourself, "What can I do to make this relationship work?"

Relationships and Accounting Don't Do Well Together

It's common for couples to keep score, and some type of balance sheet in check in their relationship. Forget scoring, because marriage is not a balance sheet. Forget "all the past credits" you've accumulated, even though you feel you have earned your points, and it's simply not fair to forget all this, and start from scratch. This thinking doesn't work. If it did, obviously you wouldn't have come to this point.

Are You a Frog?

There is another reason why you should change (first). If you are experiencing problems in your relationship right now, most likely those problems have been accumulating over some period of time.

Maybe you're familiar with the story of the frog that found himself in a pot filled with water. A slow fire was burning beneath, so the water in the pot was warming up slowly. It was warming up so slowly that each time the frog said "Damn, it's getting hot in here," it wasn't much worse than the last time, so the frog decided to do nothing about it. Things went on like this for quite a while, and every time the temperature rose, the frog thought that it wasn't so bad after all. Well, as you can imagine, things evolved to a point where it didn't matter anymore what the frog thought, because it got ... hmm, cooked.

So, are you a frog?

If not, act now. The time to act is now. Someone has to take the lead right now, and that is you. And by the way, you're doing that already. You are taking the lead right now by reading this book, and maybe some other books, as well. The important thing to remember is that the work will not be finished by reading this book. Rather, it's only the beginning.

You will have to act on it. Take the lead!

Sometimes Bad Things Happen to Good People

Another thing common in successful marriages is that the couples maintain high standards for their marriage.

- They have high expectations of each other.
- They do not settle for average.

- They don't let things slide.
- They don't give up and live in apathy or think, "This is the way it should be."
- They are vigilant in their relationships, and make sure their love juice doesn't get too many toxic ingredients mixed in it.

Most people think that if you do a poor job, you get poor results. You do a good job, you get good results. If you do an excellent job, well, then you get excellent results.

To me, this is wrong. This is not how the world spins, though I wish it did. I believe this is as valid for marriage and relationships, as well.

What I have just said is something that Tony Robbins teaches, and who has taught me a couple of things in life. This is one of them. The principle is equally valid for anything that you do, but in terms of marriage and relationships, I believe it's even more important, because we are talking about the most important thing that you do in life-spending your life with another human being, who you love and want to grow old with, and who has a huge impact on how successful you'll be in life.

I believe what really happens is this: You do a poor job—you get nothing, and your partner leaves you. You do a good job—you get poor results. Most people are good people. There is no sarcasm here. Most of the time, people do a good job. They try as hard as they can. They juggle the demands of everyday life to the best of their ability. If anyone were to ask them how they feel about their performance in their relationship, they'd say that they do a reasonably good job, and they didn't deserve the troubles they have.

Then again, why do so many bad things happen to good people? Why are good people living in miserable relationships, feeling unhappy and unfulfilled? Why are good people left alone?

It seems so unfair. And it is. I'm sorry to say this, but I believe that doing a good job just isn't good enough these days. Doing a good jobs means that your relationship is somewhere in the middle of your priorities. Doing *only* a good job means you will get not-so-good or poor results.

On the other hand, if you do an excellent job, you'll get good results. And if you do an outstanding job, then you may enjoy extraordinary results, reaping rewards big time. In terms of relationships, I think you should be shooting for no less than an excellent and outstanding job. Even though it sounds intimidating, I believe you can do it. I believe everyone can do it.

You may be thinking, "How am I supposed to do an excellent job?" I say, one step at a time. You'll get there. Your relationship didn't get to the stage it's in now in one day, so it will take some time to get it back to balance. As a matter of fact, you're already on your way.

If you are serious about your goals, and your vision of your marriage, by now your brain already has a new direction. This is great news because, from now on, nothing can stop you from doing an excellent job in your relationship. So, fasten your seat belt and get ready.

Grab Your Feel Good Glasses

Couples who are in trouble frequently have forgotten about the good things in their relationships.

When this happens they often:

- Only see things that are "wrong," of course, not with them, but with their partner.
- They give no credit or signs of appreciation to each other.
- They have the "All is on me" syndrome.

Maybe you focus on what doesn't work rather than what works as well. If so, you are leaving the most precious aspects of your relationship completely out of your mental picture.

Is it fair to your spouse? Is it fair to you? Does it make you more or less happy? Think about it.

Spending time together only complaining and telling your partner what they don't do right, how bad they really are, having your partner feel like an idiot, will only drive your partner away.

Even worse, it might lead your partner to stay, yet hate you for the rest of your lives. What is worse; it's for you to decide, but the real question is, do you want that?

If you truly want your partner to listen and hear and understand what you are saying then, for starters, stop complaining about your partner and start talking about you first.

Talk about how you feel. When you succeed in doing this little change, your partner will start listening and, most importantly, hearing what you have to say much more easily.

You Live With Another Person

Surprise! You and your spouse are different people. While this is obvious, it's also something we have a hard time remembering.

People used to believe that the earth was flat, and they would fall off if they came to the end of it. Well, as we all know, that is not true, but at the time, it was the map of the world of the people from that time in history.

Why is this important and what does it have to do with your relationship?

It's important for you to realize that everything you think, believe, hold value to, what you do and how you communicate to others is influenced by your particular map of the world, your view of the world. The same goes for your partner. Okay, so where is the problem?

The problem is not that we have a map of the world, but that we forget we have one.

Most couples assume they see things alike. When it becomes clear that this is not the case, they begin to "change" the other's view to make it fit their map of the world. If your maps are significantly different, it will be very difficult to understand each other, as you literally don't understand what the other is saying.

The Map is Not the Territory

The concept that the map is not the territory (a phrase first coined by Alfred Korzybski) is one of the ideas that laid the foundation of Neuro-Linguistic Programming (NLP) that was created by Dr. Richard Bandler and Dr. John Grinder. It's important for you to realize that your map of the world is incomplete. In other words, what's on your map doesn't necessarily correspond fully to what's truly out there. The map is not the territory.

What do I mean?

In order to understand the world, we map it in our brains. It helps us process information without being overloaded. Maps of the world are not good or bad, they simply are. But as said, they are incomplete. They don't hold all the information.

Why not?

To keep it simple, I'll borrow an example from Dr. Richard Bandler because it makes it easy to understand how a map of the world is formed in our brains. So, let us imagine a city map. To make a map of the world in our mind, we basically go through three basic steps.

We delete

On a city map, we don't draw the cars, and we don't know what the rooftops look like, right? This is highly useful, because it would be too much to hold all that information. Well, it's useful until you delete something important, like a whole block of buildings, and then try to drive through them because your map says there's nothing there. Think how many times you have experiences like this. You're walking down a familiar street and all of a sudden, you notice a new shop. You walk in, ask how long it's been open, and find out it's been there for five years! You just didn't notice it before because you'd deleted that part of the information. Think how this translates do your relationship. Are you missing something because you think it's not there? You might not se the good stuff you have together because your maps shows it's nothing there. Is it?

We generalize

On a map, state roads are represented by the same color, regardless of what the particular roads actually look like. Also, when we see a blue-colored shape on a map, we expect it to be a lake or the sea. This actually is how we learn things. You play with fire, you get burned, and so you learn not to touch things when they are hot. This is a good thing. But again, it's not always so useful. Let's say you have a partner who cheated on you, so you decide all men are pigs. That might be a slight over-generalization, don't you think?

We distort

Lastly, we distort part of the information that gets to our brains. A city map is usually a smaller piece of paper, smaller than the city itself, right? And it's also flat as it's printed on a piece of paper. We do the same with our map of the world. A good indicator that we have distorted information is how we blow things out of proportion or we make them bigger or smaller than they actually are. Another, subtler way we distort things is that we attach a meaning to something that happened, or something that someone said or did. Your spouse enters the room and she doesn't greet you. You figure she must be angry or upset. You might be right, but maybe not.

I don't mean to say that distortion is necessarily a bad thing. What is important though is that you realize that it's there, and that it's a process that is going on in your head as well as in the head of your partner. It's important to realize that the way you see things, and the way they really are, are not necessarily the same thing. Actually, many times they are not. Whatever you think is going on, it's just your map. And it doesn't necessarily match the map of your spouse and others.

So, next time you end up arguing, or thinking in your head who's right or who's wrong, think about that. As long as you stay with your own map, you'll stay convinced that you're probably right. And your spouse will stay convinced that he is probably right. When your map and the map of your spouse don't match, that's when the trouble begins.

So, what's the truth? Who's right, then?

It's not about who's right and who's wrong. It's not about what's true either. A good map gets you to see things from a different perspective, and that gives you ultimate freedom.

Once you fully realize that, you'll also understand that in order to have better feelings and better interactions with your partner, you'll need to expand you map of the world with your partner's map. You'll have to familiarize yourself with a map of your partner as much as possible with as much detail as possible. When you do, you are suddenly able to see things from your partner's point of view, and this makes a huge difference. It's then that you are able to achieve lasting changes in your relationship.

In human history, many wars began simply because leaders of the opposite sides had mismatching maps of the world, and they didn't bother to get to know each other better before they started a war. If you don't want to constantly be in a war with your partner, you need to get to know your partner's map of the world better. Worry not, after you finish this book, you'll know how to do it, so stay tuned.

The Silent Killer of Your Relationship

Many experts claim that if you have trouble in your relationship, you have to fix your communication. I agree. Yet, I don't believe that bad communication is a reason for trouble in a relationship.

I believe that the real, and many times overlooked, killer of relationships is a negative perception of our partners, and the relationship in general.

How you perceive your partner (and yourself) creates many more problems than poor communication itself. It's the negative perception fed by malicious focus on the "wrong" parts of your partner's personality that is killing the relationship.

So what exactly do I mean by perception?

It's how we see things. It's what we believe about our partner to be true. It doesn't matter if this belief matches the reality. In your map of the world, this is true and, with time, you are getting more and more convinced of it.

Now, if you believe that your partner is the most capable person in the world, that's great. Even though this belief could be questioned somewhat by a neutral person, it's a good belief, as it serves your relationship in a good sense. All that matters is that it's true for YOU.

On the other hand, if your perception of your partner is that he is, for example, sloppy, then this is true for you, as well, but it's not so useful anymore. The problem with negative perceptions of our partners is that they are self-reinforcing. Which brings us to the next point.

If you remember, earlier in the book, we said that each person has his or her own map of the world. In other words, we can say that every person applies their own unique set of lenses through which they see things. Those lenses are powerful mental filters at work.

Filters are very powerful because, by definition, they let in only proofs that support your belief about your spouse.

They work both ways. When you are in love, there isn't a single person on the face of this planet who could convince you that your newly found mate isn't the funniest person, even though many other people would disagree.

On the other hand, if you believe your spouse is sloppy, you will notice socks left on the floor once, but you won't pay attention to the many times when this doesn't happen. You will see only the dirty dishes, but you will not see the lawn meticulously cut like the finest Persian carpet. You will literally delete all the information that goes against your belief.

Once you are convinced of something, it's really hard to change that conviction except when something dramatic happens, like sickness, divorce or death. It's when we are about to lose something that we begin to appreciate what we have.

My question to you is this: Do we have to experience dramatic events to start thinking about our spouse's strengths, and things we like and enjoy?

Smart couples act, and don't rely on dramatic events such as divorce (which is death of an intimate relationship) to remind them how precious their partner really is. They don't wait for that very moment when they realize that they have actually lost their partner only to remember again what they once had. This would be plain stupid, yet it's astonishing how many couples do just that.

Your Feel Good GPS

Before you are tempted to skip this chapter, I ask you not to. Why? Because your brain desperately needs direction. Knowing what you want from your marriage is that direction and, as such, a foundation for everything else we are going to talk about here. It's your relationship's North Star.

Successful couples have a common vision, and a sense for a shared purpose in their marriage, and they can describe it accurately. A good and tested approach to create a vision of your marriage together will be discussed toward the end of this book, but now, let's focus on you. After all, it's with you where everything starts.

When asked, many people have some idea what they want, but more often than not, they know much better what they don't want. This is not a good approach. That's because it drives you away from something instead of focusing your mind on something.

On the other hand, all successful people do things in a similar way. I have found the same to be true for marriages and relationships too.

1. They know what they want.
2. They know why they want it.

3. They are convinced they can and will achieve what they want.

4. They can be convinced, because they know exactly how they will achieve their goal. They either already have the necessary knowledge, skills and experience, or they know exactly how they'll learn.

5. They do something about it every single day.

6. They persist. If things don't work, they change the approach and try something else.

7. They celebrate their successes, and have fun along the way.

Many people take shortcuts and omit some steps. For example, many people set goals, and they can explain why it matters to them. Why is it then that so many New Year's resolutions are dropped after only a week? The problem is that people may very well know why they want something, but deep down inside, they don't believe that they can and will achieve it. They are not convinced. Then there are people who are falsely convinced. They lack the knowledge, skills and experience, and are not even aware of it.

For example, you may have absolute clarity that you want to watch the sunset because it makes you feel good watching it. You may also be convinced you can pull it off. But you are looking east. And you wonder why there is no sunset. No matter how much clarity you have in what you want and why you want it, no matter how convinced you are that you can pull it off, no one has ever seen the sunset looking east. You lack the knowledge that it's the west you should be looking toward. You didn't apply the right method. That's called education.

Wise couples educate themselves constantly. They find out what worked for other people, modify it to suit their needs, and take it from there.

Then there are people who've gotten everything right so far, but lack the discipline to actually execute it. Henry Ford used to say, "Vision without execution is just hallucination." Successful couples don't hallucinate. They make their vision come true by actually doing something about it.

The last step that people omit, including myself years ago, is they forget to celebrate their successes and have fun. We are not machines, and we achieve goals faster and with greater energy if we make things fun. It's really important to reward yourself for the good things you have done, for changes you have achieved in your life, and in your relationship. And it doesn't have to be a fancy dinner or something expensive. You can celebrate in your mind first by simply reminding yourself that there is something you can be proud of. A good way to do this is journaling, which is something I do, as well. It's my way to have some reflection over the successes I've had, including all those little magical moments that make life in a relationship so beautiful, but are so easily forgotten. Even though journaling is beyond the topic of this book, I have a couple of useful tips related to it toward the end of the book.

Why is getting direction for your brain so important?

Imagine the GPS navigation system you have in your car or on your phone. If you put in an exact address, the device will lead you exactly where you want to go. And if you get lost or get off track, the system will recalculate and prepare a new route for you. So, while the goal or the target remains the same, because the conditions have changed, the plan has changed as well. This is what we mean by changing the approach and keep trying.

Let's now imagine, while still using the same navigation device, you do not know where you want to go. Well, as we all know, even the best GPS navigation device will not be able to help you.

Ask yourself, "What will I put in my relationship's GPS navigation device? What's my goal?"

Clarity gives power to make the right decisions, and the inner strength to do whatever needs to be done. It's that inner strength and determination, that some call faith, that determines if you will find your way around obstacles in life, and troubles in marriage, or get stuck at the first obstacle that comes your way.

Remember, you don't need to know every little step that you need to take along your way. That is not possible, and also not necessary, as the GPS device will adjust your route according to the new route calculation if you go off track. But you have to know where you want to go.

Knowing what you want from your marriage is not enough. You have to know WHY you want it. Why is this so important to you? Because the answer to that "why" is actually your internal drive, and the main reason why you do it anyway. It's your internal driving force that doesn't let anything get in the way. It's your North Star. It's also your safety belt, which holds you firmly in your life's driver's seat when your marital road gets bumpy, and others give up. You won't. You'll hold your driving wheel firmly and persist.

Personally, I believe that if you know what your goals are, and why you want to achieve them, you are way ahead of 95 percent of the rest of the people. If you can imagine your goals vividly, so you know exactly how they look, feel and sound when you have achieved them, then you have just set yourself up a big and bright North Star, something that only a small portion of people actually have. And if you haven't set up your North Star, you can do it now!

Even if you get lost or some clouds get in the way, the next time you look up, it's going to be there, your North Star, brightly leading you toward your goal.

Exercise

Set some time aside when you won't get disturbed. Take a sheet of paper and a pencil, turn off your phone and emails, and relax. Now ask yourself:

1. What do I want from my relationship?

- What do I want to think of my relationship before I die?
- If I had a magic stick, and could have an outstanding marriage, how would it look?
- Write your thoughts in the form of statements. Be short and as specific as you can. Put your statements in a table like the example below.

2. For each of those statements ask yourself:

- Why is this important to me?
- Why does it matter?
- Write the answers down next to the statements from number 1.

3. For each statement, imagine that you have already achieved your goals. Write down everything that you see, feel and hear.

4. For each statement, think what will happen if you don't achieve a goal. Write this down as well.

What do I want?	Why does it matter?	What do I see, or feel when I am there?	What happens if I don't achieve this goal?

5. When you're done, reread it. You'll need it later in the book.

6. Don't worry if you feel that something is missing. You'll get ideas later in the book. Just keep that sheet of paper somewhere handy so you can add things as you go along.

Note:

You can download a ready-made My Feel-Good GPS printable worksheet from your members area.

http://geni.us/fgmbonus

Set Your Relationship's Metabolism
to Feel Good

Let's talk about losing weight for a minute, and the ever-present desire to lose weight permanently. Those of you who have managed to do it, know very well that the real "secret" (even though it's not really a secret) to losing weight permanently is to change your metabolism.

It's not just eating healthier and less, but also working out regularly and making a habit of it. That's all there is to it. That's why you'll often hear that, in order to permanently lose weight, you have to change your lifestyle. In my own experience, that's true. That's when your efforts and the dieting start having a lasting effect. Otherwise, your body will do its best to get back to your previous weight, one way or another.

In terms of your relationship, you want that positive, lasting effect as well. It's about lasting change, and not just temporarily feeling better because of a week without the kids, and a couple of good books on a remote beach under the tropical sun (although that wouldn't hurt once in a while). Similar to losing weight permanently, it means changing the metabolism of your relationship.

You have to change the way you digest your thoughts, and how you think about each other. It's how you perceive your partner, the way you feel about your marriage and your partner, and the way you behave. And the way to do it is by regular action, not as a coincidence, but as a deliberate act.

This is why love is not an act of having, but an act of doing.

The easiest way to start changing your relationship's metabolism is in how you treat each other and how you think about each other, creating a friendly atmosphere.

Why?

Taking into account what you know about the human brain now, you know that if people feel criticized, disliked, unappreciated, judged or rejected by another, their brains perceive this as danger. They feel under siege, and dig in to protect themselves. And then it's impossible for anyone to achieve real change. So what you want to achieve first is for you and your partner to feel safe, respected, understood and loved. This is what we are going to do in the next chapter.

Start Creating
a Feel Good Atmosphere

It doesn't sound sexy, but you have to be friends first before expecting to be in a healthy, happy and long-lasting relationship.

Therefore, this part of the book explains how to (re)connect, create and sustain a friendly and safe atmosphere, *a feel good atmosphere* for both of you.

While it sounds a bit ambiguous, the good news is that creating a friendly atmosphere is actually the easiest part. That is why it's placed at the beginning of this book. Also, it allows baby steps that, from my experience, are the most effective at changing behaviors.

Becoming friends with your spouse means:

- Focusing on what's working and starting to appreciate the good stuff. Right now you might not remember any, but believe me there is plenty. I'll help you discover it.

- Stopping taking the posion pills. This means ending all negativity, especially criticism, sarcasm and giving silent treatments.

- Doing nice, little things for each other. Surprising each other.

- Spending time together on purpose and regularly, just the two of you. Time when you talk about your relationship, and time when you just have fun. Time when you are tender to each other. Time used for getting to know each other better. You will be surprised how many things you still don't know about your spouse.

How do you do that in a way that is natural and not intimidating? How can you do that without having to transform yourself into another person in a day?

So, let's start creating a friendly atmosphere now. We'll start with things that don't require cooperation from your spouse. Therefore, you can begin putting this advice into practice today.

Focus on What's Working

All couples have good stuff. But too many times, they just forget that. It's all too easy to get stuck with all your mental filters and negative perceptions of each other, to not see the good stuff anymore. I know, I was there with my wife, and I know it's not pleasant, to put it mildly.

Negative thoughts trigger negative feelings, and negative feelings lead to negative behaviors, such as anger, aggressiveness or avoidance, to name just a few. Negative behaviors inevitably lead to negative results, such as divorce or leading separate lives under the same roof, while sharing the kids and finances, whichever you think is worse.

In our society we spend way too much time thinking about what's wrong, instead of focusing on what's okay, and then building on that. We do the same in our relationships.

It doesn't have to be that way. Successful couples find lots and lots of reasons to share joy, love, appreciation and positivity with each other. They know that they have to be grateful for many beautiful things in their relationship. It's easy to forget that. If your marriage is struggling, it may have been a long, long time since you thought about anything positive in your relationship, let alone shared this with your spouse.

It's interesting how quickly we start taking things for granted, including relationships. Yet, it's lack of gratitude, and the awareness of many beautiful things in our lives, that cause us to focus on things that don't work, and overlook the brighter side, and the many other things that work wonderfully.

It's also interesting how quickly we tend to change that perception once we are about to lose something that, five minutes before, we took for granted. It seems like something dramatic has to happen in order for us to start looking at our relationship differently. It seems like someone has to get really sick, if not die, for our perspective to shift. Then, things that once used to be extremely important and would drive us mad, in the face of possible death, suddenly become irrelevant. In such moments when we realize that we are about to lose something, or someone, or may have lost already, it hits us hard.

You don't want to wait for that moment to happen in order to start turning things around for the better, do you?

There has to be an easier way. No one has to get sick or seriously injured in order for you to start showing some gratitude toward the people you love, your spouse and lastly to yourself and your life. Do you agree?

So let's do something about it.

Exercise

For just three minutes, I want you to put everything else aside, and give your marriage a quick boost by completing the statements below.

Note: A ready-made 3-Minute Relationship Booster worksheet is waiting for you in your members download area.

http://geni.us/fgmbonus

Now think about your partner and write down at least five things for each of the questions below.

1. I like your

_____

(curly red hair, brown eyes, soft / strong hands, softness of your lips)

2. I admire your

_____

(energy, passion for_____, sense of humor, imagination,

courage to_____, ability to_____, kindness, patience,

sense of order)

3. I really like _____/ What I really appreciate about you

is_____

(You are so patient when I freak out, your fabulous cooking, how
you kiss me, the way you touch me, when you open the door of the
car for me, how you always organize our vacation without a flaw,
how you keep our home cozy, you being prepared to step back, you
being such a good mother/father)

4. I like watching you when you are

_____

(smiling, naked, in a business suit, walking, reading fairy tales to the
kids, telling jokes, cooking, teaching the kids to play ball)

5. Thank you.

Maybe you haven't been able to find five positive things for each
question, especially if you are fighting a lot. If that's the case, don't
worry. There are more than five things for sure, but you just don't
see them yet. Your perception of your spouse still employs a very
powerful filter. It's the filter that distorts the truth. Just put the
current findings and the list somewhere safe, and come back later. In

the meantime, actively look for the good traits and positive things in your relationship, and take notes.

There is of course a purpose behind all this. You need to change your thoughts about your partner so you can change your feelings about him or her. Only then will you have a chance to change the behaviors and actions that led you to this situation in the first place.

And there is another part to this exercise. Now, you have to tell this to your partner. Yes, you heard me right. Then watch the change on your partner's face.

Yes, it might feel odd. It will. But remember, it's for the greater cause. Just think, when will you feel more embarrassed and odd? Once you divorce? Or now when your job is to just tell your partner that you appreciate and love so many things about him! It's something that you probably haven't shared with him for such a long time! I can guarantee you, your partner will NOT complain about that!

Then again, if you still can't tell your partner, that's fine. Just have your letter somewhere handy. It's a reminder of the good things, and that is what I want you to achieve here.

Now, go to your journal and report what you are feeling. You might have something interesting to write about.

Stop Taking the Poison Pills

There will always be some things that we are not satisfied with, including our spouses. But in a healthy relationship, discontent and anger should only be expressed in a disciplined and structured manner.

Here I will name the three most harmful practices that are common for couples in trouble. The practices I am going to talk about are like poison pills for any relationship. If you recognize some of these to be present in your relationship, you have to stop immediately, even if it's only you who stops.

Criticism

The main difference between complaining and criticism is that criticism is aimed at your partner's character or personality as a whole. With criticism, the blame is placed on the person and not the behavior of that person. Also, criticism tends to have a recurring pattern, making it even more damaging.

The easiest way you can recognize criticism is by watching for phrases containing the word "you" typically followed by a generalization such as always, ever, never, nothing, or all, or such that are implied in the meaning.

Some examples:

- Why can't you be on time just once? I just can't rely on you!
- Why can't you ever remember anything?

- All the work is on me (you never do anything).

- What is wrong with you (all the time)? Why do you have to be so sloppy (all the time)?

Why is criticizing not working?

It's a fact that people can change only if they feel that they are genuinely liked and accepted as they are. When people feel criticized, disliked and unappreciated, they are unable to change. Instead, their amygdala is alert, and the conscious part of their minds shuts off. The only thing they think of is to dig in to protect themselves or fight back.

Criticism is also hypnotic because of its highly repetitive nature. When we criticize, we usually repeat our criticism in exactly the same way over and over again. "Why can't you ever …?" repeated hundreds of times becomes a suggestion and a "command" to the subconscious mind.

In that sense, if you criticize, you in fact hypnotize the other person into behaving exactly the opposite of how you'd like them to. Think of that the next time you have an urge to criticize someone.

In this book, you will learn how to avoid criticism, and express your annoyance in a more productive way. Also, you'll learn how to handle criticism aimed at you.

Sarcasm

Sarcasm comes in various forms, but the most common is when someone is deliberately trying to make their spouse feel bad, stupid, incompetent, lazy, disorganized, _____ (insert appropriate feeling), often disguised as humor.

Not surprisingly, the origin of the word sarcasm derives from the Greek word *sarkazein*, which literally means, "to tear or strip off the flesh." The Greeks obviously knew that because—it does hurt.

The underlying issue of sarcasm is disrespect. When you lose respect for another human being, it's then that your relationship with that person is in big danger. If this is your partner, they will feel it all too well as it attacks their self-esteem and self-worth.

Some people go even further. They make sarcastic comments to their spouses in front of their common friends. Despite smiling outwardly, the person on the receiving end feels put down and humiliated. Some people don't stop there, as they'll make poisonous, sarcastic comments in front of their children. To be sarcastic myself, it's a great way to teach children about relationships.

Often, couples are being mutually sarcastic. It's kind of a vicious game inflicting wounds on each other to make it even "for the last time." Those couples probably have never asked themselves if that is what will bring them closer to what they want.

Exercise

- Consciously observe what in your relationship is working just fine, if not great. Try to remember that. Better yet, put it in your journal.

- Each day, tell your partner what you appreciated about him or her that day. Many times, we think in our head, yet we don't say it. Share it with your spouse. I haven't seen a single person who would bite because others were praising them.

- For the next week, be especially vigilant about words like always, never, nothing, and replace them with sometimes, last time, yesterday, last week ... In short, replace generalizations with specifics. Notice how many times you would have sounded criticizing to your partner, and how you didn't, solely because of this small exercise.

- When you are tempted to say a sarcastic comment, bite your tongue.

Silent treatments

Silent treatments also called stonewalling, is a behavior pattern that happens to couples who usually already have a long history of bad relationship habits behind them.

It builds on:

- A history of criticism
- The lack of energy for yet another fight
- An inability to apologize mindfully

In absence of other more productive means to solve the conflict, it's a way to "punish" the other partner by not communicating.

The silent treatment is not a productive way to communicate disagreement, because it doesn't solve anything, and it leaves the other partner wondering about its cause, with a high probability that it will be misinterpreted.

I used to do this as my way of showing I was not content with something my wife had done. Seeing that she didn't intend to apologize, and me not wanting to end up in yet another fight, I would give my wife the silent treatment that would last for days.

In the meantime, I would limit my interactions with my wife to a bare minimum. If we did talk, it would be about the children, like who was going to pick them up at school, or maybe something else important. Aside from that, I would show a "cold" behavior, uninterested, reserved and do my thing.

And all the time, I would be nurturing and spinning negative thoughts about my wife, thinking about negative traits of her personality, and how all this contributed to the mess.

I did that until I learned how damaging it is. It tells your partner you don't care. It sends the "I no longer care for your feelings" message.

Silence is communication as well, as it sends a message of rejection. Even though we may, of course, care for our partner, when we are giving the silent treatment, our partner's brain perceives it as if we don't care anymore. If we do it often enough, our partner's brain will start believing that. When this happens, we have a much bigger problem then we thought.

Exercise

- Think of the last time you gave your partner the silent treatment.
- Remember why it happened, and how you reacted.
- Now, think as if you are already successful at implementing what you've learned so far.
- Imagine your different self. Imagine how you'd do it differently.
- What would you say? What would you do?

Silence the Evil Voices in Your Head

It's generally a bad plan to nurture negative self-talk about your partner, yet people do that, and then wonder why they can't fix their relationship.

If I came into your living room, and painted on your biggest wall a giant picture of your evil spouse, would you want to live there? Hell no! So why do you allow yourself to have one in your head?

Bad thoughts will make you feel bad, and you cannot be pleasant to your partner when you feel bad. Seeking a solution to a problem, while having a devil's picture with a face of your partner in your head, is impossible.

It's the Little Feel Good Things That Matter Most

Let's talk about one of the most important habits you must have for a long and happy relationship: the little things. Nice thoughts said aloud, a gentle touch, a kind smile, a sincere thank you; the little things that matter so much. Something as simple as "You make the best coffee," or "Thank you for walking the dog every night." Smiling at each other as you pass in the hall, or holding hands. Things you probably think about, but never say or do. They mean so much.

To many people, these little gestures may seem so small and unromantic. They think that lavishing big and expensive gifts and vacations on their loved ones is what they need to show how much they care. While it is wonderful to be able to enjoy fancy gifts and exotic vacations, it's a dangerous illusion to think that's all you need. It's like someone wanting to lose weight, but only dieting twice a year, or doing two push-ups per month, and expecting his body to be in perfect shape.

It's like sailing. You must constantly check your course to make sure you are still on track. If you don't, it might not make a difference at first, but after some time, you'll touch land at a completely different place. If you continue on this way, you could end up at an entirely different and unknown continent.

People who are in successful, committed relationships nourish their partnerships regularly and often. They don't set their life on cruise control, expecting a happy life. They ask themselves frequently "What can I do today to make my partner's life more pleasurable?" The little things will accumulate over time and make a huge difference.

Doing little things for each other on a regular basis can help save your marriage. It may improve your relationship enough that when a time comes where you totally mess up, forget to run that errand you promised, never called when you said you would, it won't matter as much, because you'll be in such a good place that those pesky annoyances won't seem so big. It's one of the easiest changes you can make, yet one of the most important. It's a way of changing your relationship's energy for the better. And it's crucial for every successful relationship.

Think of it as lubricant for an engine. Even the most powerful engines, casted from the best possible materials, assembled by the most skilled engineers, cannot run for long without lubricant. It helps the engine run smoothly, just as the little things help a relationship run smoothly. Think of the little things as your relationship's emollient.

Yet, it's amazing how easily we forget that the little things, those tiny tokens of appreciation, can go such a long way. Sure, it's nice to get a present for your birthday, but do you really need that stuff? Isn't it those little signs of appreciation from your partner that really make you feel accepted and loved? What's better than that warm feeling in your heart when you realize your partner is thinking about you, and did something—just because?

Do something nice and beautiful for your partner because, well, just because today you paused and thought about how lucky you are to have someone so special in your life. Because you enjoy making him feel good. Because you know it will make her feel loved.

If your relationship is in trouble, chances are you stopped doing the little things for each other a long time ago. Many couples complain about how they always fight, and how angry they are at one another. But by trying to do the little things, you and your partner can begin to turn things around.

For the remainder of this chapter, I'm going to talk more about the importance of the little things, and I want to give you some suggestions for things you can start doing to better your relationship.

What Exactly Are These "Little Things"?

There are many relationship books that say couples should share chores, or do the work for the other. They're right. Sharing chores is absolutely essential in a successful relationship. Gone are the days when it was the wife who stayed at home, while her man went off to work. In many relationships today, both partners work, so it's important to share the burden at home. It's also a nice gesture to do the chores for your partner once in a while, just because. And it's also nice to swap chores. You'll both gain an appreciation for the work that the other does.

While sharing chores will help your relationship, it's not enough. After all, life together isn't just about who's doing what chores. That would be boring, and quite sad. You also need the little things:

- Say "Thank you"
- Kiss your partner lovingly when he or she leaves home
- Smile when you meet again
- Give a big hug
- Give a loving look directly into your partner's eyes
- Gently touch when passing your partner
- Tell you partner how much you appreciate him or her
- Send your spouse a loving text message in the middle of the day
- Invite your partner to lunch
- Rub his neck when he sits behind the desk
- Giving a foot massage when watching television together
- Leave a love note in her wardrobe
- Put a love note with a piece of candy in his suitcase before a trip

- Guys – open her car door (Still remember how that goes??)
- Order something from a catalogue she looks at

Here are some ideas that take a little more planning, but are worth it:

- Wake up first and prepare breakfast with your partner's favorite cereal
- Prepare a breakfast in bed on Sunday morning
- Before you head out, leave his or her favorite coffee on the table
- Leave a glass of fresh squeezed orange juice on the counter to make sure your spouse starts the day with a vitamin boost
- Pick a chore that your partner routinely does and do it yourself, without your partner knowing, and without any expectations of thanks

This is an excerpt from the list of things my wife loves that I do for her:

- On Mondays and Wednesdays, buying her favorite women's magazines
- Giving her a neck massage when she had a stressful day
- Paying bills for her (She really hates doing it herself)
- Filling up the gas tank of her car.
- Giving her a foot massage when we watch television together

- The most difficult for me: not being anxious while she shops. Personally, I don't like shopping, but I try to be accommodating and pleasant. It means a lot to her.

There's more!

In your members area you'll find the golden collection of 47 simple little things you can do for your spouse to show your thoughtfulness and caring in a most natural way.

We call them the *love boosters* because they cost no money and take just a tiny fraction of your time. You can start right now because they don't require cooperation from your partner.

http://geni.us/fgmbonus

Surprise and mystery

You may not be aware of this, but surprising your spouse is a powerful aphrodisiac. Esther Perel, a French researcher who dedicated her professional life to exploring erotic desire, found that surprises and mysteries are one of the core elements of desire. Our brains look for familiarity, but love surprises. That is why people can't resist affairs. They're thrilling because they're new, and they make people feel alive. Make your partner feel alive with surprises you create. It's a much better plan than doing nothing, in which case, eventually someone else may show up to fill the void.

Create a list of surprises that would delight your partner, and give him or her one, at least once a month and at different times and days to keep it unexpected.

Call up your babysitter, make a reservation at your favorite restaurant and invite your partner to a surprise dinner.

When your partner returns home from a business trip, prepare your bedroom with candles and massage oil, and give him or her a nice massage.

Watch your partner closely and learn what makes him or her happy or excited. Return to the store and purchase that item your partner fancied when window-shopping.

Pay attention to the look on her face when she sees something she likes. Last summer, my wife and I were strolling through the beautiful Italian town of Peschiera del Garda, doing some window-shopping. My wife saw a belt that she thought would go perfectly with her favorite jeans, but the shop had closed for the night. The following day, I made an excuse to go out. I snuck down to that shop and bought the belt my wife wanted. I gave it to her at a dinner we were having the following week. It was such a great surprise!

Pay attention to small wishes. Listen when your partner makes a comment about something on television. One evening, my wife saw a nice handbag on television, and it piqued my interest as well, as it looked nice even to me, a non-expert on women's handbags. I secretly took a picture of the television screen with my phone, and stored it away. It came in handy about five months later when my wife's birthday was approaching. Of course she didn't expect such a present and her loving look was more than worth the effort.

Why are doing little things for each other so important?

The most obvious reason is that you make your partner happy. Yes, it's that simple and that powerful. But there is another, even more powerful element at play here: your inner voice. Notice that your mind becomes much more forgiving and understanding, and that alone is worth pure gold.

What do I mean by your inner voice? When you do little things for your spouse, you build up positive interactions between one another. It's like making small deposits of money to your bank account every day, but in this case, it's your emotional account. Your, as some might call it, Love Bank or Love Account. It doesn't matter what you call it as long as you understand what I'm talking about. What does matter is what research shows us. Couples who've stayed together have five times more positive interactions than negative ones. I believe this is true. It's what saved my own marriage when it was in trouble and we weren't sure of what to do next.

Doing little things for one another
is your best insurance policy for a successful relationship.

It's the lubricant that will keep it from getting rusty. It's keeping your love machine in shape so that when troubles comes along, like a stable boat graciously rolling over the waves, your relationship will ride the tide and continue on its forward and upward direction.

Though, unlike many insurance policies, you can't pay in advance or at the end of the year. You must keep paying small amounts day by day, month by month, year after year, in order for this insurance policy to work.

Difficult times and events will come and go, but the important thing is how you handle them. There will be times when you'll get uneasy with your partner, or you'll have negative feelings about something your partner did or said. No matter how many books on improving your relationship you read, there will be times when you might explode, and start a nasty fight, despite what you've learned.

But, because of the many positive interactions you've created with your partner, you'll be much more inclined to give them the benefit of the doubt when you get angry. You'll be more likely to be forgiving, and tell yourself that, "Hey, we're fine. This is just a minor issue and we'll resolve it in time. I love him/her." And it's because, on a regular basis, you are given proof that your partner thinks about you, cares how you feel and genuinely wants you to feel good, by doing those little things for you.

This is why good friends are good friends. They have had so many pleasant experiences together that when they argue over something or occasionally become offended by something the other might have said, it isn't reason enough to break up the friendship. They'll make up and remain good friends because they have invested in positive experiences together. Going out, doing fun things, or simply calling each other on the phone and discussing things, telling each other secrets, and doing small favors for one another; all the stuff that good friends do. With all those little things, their ties grow stronger every day. This is what you want to achieve in your relationship.

Things to Keep in Mind

Never expect something in return. Do it for your partner, do it because you'll make your spouse happy! Do it for your partner's smile and loving look. Do it even if your spouse doesn't notice. And even when he does, do something else again.

Feeling a bit uneasy about starting this, maybe even a little embarrassed? Maybe you fear your partner might ask what's wrong. Just remember that nothing can be wrong with doing something nice for each other.

The worst thing that could happen is your partner won't notice at first. But don't worry. Your partner WILL notice. At first, your spouse might not be accustomed to these things. But once your partner knows for sure that these acts of kindness are not a coincidence, you will see a change.

Your partner might ask you at first, "Is something wrong?" or perhaps suggests, "This is not like you." That's great! Don't say anything, or maybe just say, "Nothing. I just remembered how much I love you."

Make a list of ideas and keep it handy for when you need a quick peep, or want to amend it as soon as you get an idea.

I keep a list of the little things my wife likes, and a list of gift ideas. For this I use Evernote, a mobile application for note taking, but you can use a piece of paper that you keep in your wallet just as well. It's convenient to use an app because it's always with you on your phone, and you can easily add to the list. Sometimes I might get an idea and I'll email it to myself, possibly with a picture or a recording.

Exercise

- Make a list of 10 things you can do that you know will make your partner happy.

- Be specific.

- Use ideas I've mentioned if you can't think of any. You'll soon be coming up with your own.

- Commit to saying something nice and doing nice things for your spouse every day.

- Commit to surprising your spouse at least once a month.

- Observe what your spouse likes, which will give you new ideas.

- Expand the list as time goes by.

- Persist. Show your love by example and not by words alone.

Take Time to Feel Good Together

Let me begin with a question. How important is your relationship to you? The fact that you are reading this book makes me believe it's very important. And when asked, most people would answer the same. But is it really so?

Answer the following questions:

- How much time do you spend with your partner each day?
- Of that time, how much is taken up with doing chores or things around the house?
- How much time do you spend in the same room, but doing separate things?
- How many minutes on average in a day do you engage in an actual conversation where you are actively listening to one another and maintaining eye contact?
- Of that time, how many minutes do you talk about things other then your kids, your jobs, the house, and maybe parents?
- How many minutes per week?

I've asked these questions because I'm sure that you said your relationship is very important. But people's lives don't reflect what they say. I find it much more accurate to look at how couples spend their time together, their energy and their money. Relationships shouldn't be about money, but they surely are about time and energy.

There are, of course, many things that we have to do on a typical day, like working, eating, taking care of the kids, paying bills, and running errands. Yet, if you said your relationship is important to you, where would you place it in relation to those activities? Only when you give your relationship a high priority can it really thrive.

Now that you've considered these questions, can you honestly say that you give your relationship its proper importance?

It's Time for Talking

I once read that the average time a couple spends together in conversation about their relationship was as little as one hour per week, and for an average couple with kids, sometimes none! By the same token, an average couple having an affair spends more than 10 hours per week together! Think about that for a moment. Those two people manage to find 10 hours or more together, in spite of possibly having their own spouses, children, and housework.

A relationship, let alone an intimate one, cannot succeed and prosper on three and a half minutes per day. It's not enough meaningful communication. It's astonishing to me how little time the average couple devotes to talking to each other. No wonder it's also these couples who most typically have marital problems.

So how much time do you currently spend with your partner talking about the two of you? Don't count the time you talk about children, the school stuff, the house work, the repairs that need to be done, or how you're going to get your cat to stop throwing up in the bathroom sink.

It is critically important to make the time to talk to your partner, as this can determine the long-term success of your marriage. Also, it shows the priority that you are giving to your relationship. If you want to determine what really matters to someone, just look at where they're spending their money, time and energy. Taking the money factor away, do you see my point?

Make no mistake. The time for you both to talk is an intentional time, a deliberate act, a ritual on its own. It's higher than the talk you have about the kids, about stuff around the house, and about your jobs. This may sound horrible, but, to put it into perspective, would you rather have your spouse spending time with someone else for 10 hours a week?

I know it's easy for a couple to fall into this habit of not talking about their relationship. I was there. When my wife and I were at the peak of our problems, I really missed our conversations. There were times when we wouldn't have any for days. By meaningful conversations, I mean conversations as a couple, and not like two coworkers sharing the tasks of bringing money home, chores and raising children.

There are two kinds of talks that I encourage you to do. To me they are rituals in their own right, and as such have become pillars in my own marriage. I believe they are essential to any marriage and I'll explain why.

Honey, how was your day?

The first talk that I'm going to discuss is about the usual, daily conversation with the purpose of finding out how each other's day was. I call it the "Honey, how was your day?" conversation. Why is it essential to have this talk every day?

Surely you've had a friend from your youth who you've lost touch with. Maybe they moved out of town and your paths split, or you went to colleges in different parts of the country. Now imagine meeting that friend after a long period of time. It's a nice surprise and you're both happy, but it's a bit awkward, isn't it? You're not sure what to say aside from the usual "Do you have any kids?" or "Where do you work?" Why is that? Well, you just don't have any substance to talk about. You're not as close as you once were. The intimacy that you once had with your friend is now gone, and you don't have any connecting points. You're missing the dots. And the dots are exactly those everyday details that make our life interesting.

The same goes for committed relationships and marriage. If you want to have a healthy relationship, you don't want to miss the dots.

You have to know about your partner's most pressing issues, about how his life is going and what she thinks about this and that, or you will start growing apart.

There are many ways to do the "Honey, how was your day?" talk with your partner. Personally, I prefer to talk about how the day went while we're preparing dinner together. My wife will cook, and I'll chop the vegetables, or prepare the table or other things to help out. I find this to be the best experience, and I encourage you to try it. Every time we have a conversation about our days in this manner, it's so nice. It connects us, as we're preparing food together. And, by the way, have you noticed how often—out of all the available rooms in a home—people love to hang out in the kitchen?

There are many other ways you can have this important conversation, limited only by your imagination. Maybe you would rather wait until later in the evening after the kids have gone to bed. We do that often. We will sit together on the couch, and massage each other's feet, while talking about our day.

It's a tremendous stress reliever because you can vent out, but at the same time you're being touched by the person you love. On occasion, especially during the summer, we'll go out on the terrace and enjoy the warm summer evening. I'll prepare a cold drink and we'll talk.

Here are practices that I recommend you follow:

The important thing to remember is to have your "Honey, how was your day?" talk every day. Make a ritual of it.

My wife and I can have our conversation in fifteen minutes, and sometimes it can be half an hour. The point is that you must talk on a regular basis so you don't start missing the dots and missing what's up in your partner's life. You will end up living with a stranger if you allow that to happen.

Leave the television off and switch your phone to silent mode.

Don't misuse the conversation by opening issues about your relationship that you're not satisfied with. There's a time and a place for that conversation, and I'll talk about it in a bit.

When your spouse is talking, be genuinely interested.

Weave in some praise and admiration for your spouse. It feels good and it falls into the category of doing small things for your partner.

Show that you are on the same team! Even if you think your spouse is wrong, don't side with the other person. Not now. This was a mistake I did a lot. I would set my wife off visibly when I tried to be smart and objective. I learned to stop doing that. Instead, I give the support my wife needs at that moment.

Avoid giving unsolicited advice. It's highly probable that your partner just wants to be heard. Furthermore, you probably don't know all the details, so shut up, listen and offer advice only if you are asked.

I made that mistake a lot, as well. I was being so smart and I wanted to immediately offer my wife advice about what she should do to solve her problem, even though she didn't ask for it. Instead of having a husband who paid attention and listened to what she had to say, all she found at home was another smart guy telling her what to do. Don't be that person.

I realized my mistake after I noticed how much it pissed me off when my wife did the same to me. I was sometimes downright frustrated that she had a ready solution for almost all of my problems, even for things I knew she didn't have a clue about. You might say it was confidence, but I say it went straight to arguing.

These are times you'll want your partner and yourself to remember (and anchor) as something pleasant. Keep that in mind when speaking and listening. The last thing you want to do is associate this precious time of the day with unpleasant memories.

Exercise

- Start today. Ask your spouse, "How was your day?" Follow the above-mentioned principles.

- Make a ritual out of it. Remind yourself each and every day to do it. If you're afraid you might forget, put an alarm in your mobile phone's calendar. Yes, I know, it's not especially romantic, but it works.

- Have reasonable expectations. If you are reading this book by yourself and your spouse is not yet participating, follow the points above, but don't expect your spouse to ask you. It may take a while, but eventually you WILL start getting the same question in return.

Let's talk about us

Then there is the talk about your relationship. I strongly encourage you to have this conversation bi-weekly or at least once a month. I emphasize this because, from personal experience, I know how easy it is to skip this conversation. But it is crucial for the long-term health of your relationship, and I'll explain why in just a minute. This is when you set aside specific time to talk about your relationship, and your relationship only.

What do you discuss at this time?

- Reflect on what you notice about your relationship. Maybe there are things to be proud of. Maybe there are things that you are not sure about.
- Discuss how you and your partner are doing as a couple. Praise the successes in your relationship, and reflect on the times you'd handled disagreement well.
- Talk about anything that bothers you in the relationship.
- If things have been a little tense lately, this is the time to discuss why.
- Discuss disagreements calmly and in a constructive manner.
- Try to solve any major frustrations you have with one another.

Remember, this is not complaining time, but an opportunity to talk about the things in your relationship that are great, as well as the things that you would like to change for the better.

How do you start the "Let's talk about us" conversation?

Now that you know you and your partner should put away quality time to talk about your relationship, how do you begin doing that?

Sometimes couples will say, "Let's talk." Or one partner might say, "We have to talk." Hmm. That feels a bit intimidating, doesn't it? It certainly does to me. We don't know what's going to happen, and that scares us. When we hear our partner speak those words, we assume that it's not going to be pleasant.

You partner might play ignorant and ask, "About what?" as if he has no idea what's up. To diffuse the tension, you should answer with a smile and say something teasingly like, "About the political situation in Tanzania." Or, anything that might make your partner chuckle and ease his worry.

Odds are you will both smile, and the tension will ease. Then, you can say, "I was thinking about the other day, and what went on in my mind, and I'd like to tell you about it. Do you have time to sit and talk?"

Dedicate time

There is a better strategy that helps overcome the tension for good. It's what I use, and I want to recommend it to you.

Agree together to have a conversation about the relationship, and set a specific time that you can schedule in advance. You may be thinking that you have enough deadlines and schedules at work, and wonder why you need to set a fixed time to talk to your partner. Well, here are the reasons:

You know it's coming up, so you have little or no tension beforehand. You both have already agreed to the meeting, so there isn't any discomfort in asking to talk.

Scheduling a talk about your relationship in advance means that you are intentionally doing something very important. You are giving priority to your relationship.

Since you are both aware of the meeting, you can protect this time from any disruptions, such as your kids, your mother-in-law, friends or anything else that could take time away from your conversation.

My wife and I have chosen 9:00 p.m. on Sunday, and we set aside one hour so it doesn't go on too late. It doesn't matter when you meet as long as it's an undisturbed and scheduled time.

Exercise

This exercise requires your partner to participate, but if that isn't possible at the time, you can skip it, and return later when you both have the time.

It is all too easy to know how important this is, and that it must be done, and then do nothing. Therefore, I ask you to do the following:

- Find a day in the week that is likely to be the least distracting for you to have a conversation. For starters, agree to limit it to one hour and see how that goes.

- Begin your conversation by praising your partner for something, and showing your appreciation.

- Switch roles. The first time you choose the topics first, and the next time your partner chooses.

How Well Do You Know Your Partner?

Think of a best friend that you have. I don't mean people you like to hang out with, but a real friend, someone who knows almost everything about you. A friend with whom you are still able to share your deepest secrets with because you trust her, because you know she understands you and she'll be your cheerleader, no matter what you say or do. That's the kind of feeling we're looking for.

After fifteen years of marriage, I still hear new stories from my wife's past. Just the other day my wife and I went to one of our favorite places for a drink. After having asked her, my wife told me about her years in high school, a time that she hadn't shared with me in such detail before. It was magical watching her smile as she talked about that time, and it made her feel good. And because she was feeling good, it made me feel good as well. It was a simple, but well-connecting evening with my wife.

Some people say that they've grown apart. What really happened is that they haven't shared their hopes and dreams, concerns, and fears with each other for so long that they can't remember the last time they did.

No wonder they feel apart. Happy couples have detailed and intimate knowledge of their partners. Simple things like their favorite pizza topping to their innermost hopes and dreams. And they continue to learn something new about their partner every day.

You might think that nothing can surprise you about your partner anymore. I bet that is probably not true. You'll be surprised what you don't know about your partner if you ask the right questions. Questions you may never have thought to ask before. To find out more, try the following:

Exercise

- Go out and have a date with your partner. Dinner is great, but a hot chocolate around the corner and a nice walk in the park will do just as well. What's important is that you are relaxed and in a good mood.

- Follow this rule: no talking about money, children or any of your problems. Think about it as a first date; focus on learning about your partner and having fun.

- Think of questions you have never asked your partner. If you have trouble coming up with questions, pick some from the list below.

- Be curious. Encourage your partner by actively listening and saying, "Go on," "Tell me more," "How did you feel about so-and-so?" or "How did you react?"

Simple questions to ask:

- If you had 100 million dollars, what would you do? How would you spend your time? This is also a great indicator of what your partner's vision is of their life and relationship. Simple, yet powerful.

- If you had 24 hours left to live, what would you do and why?

- What was your favorite television show when you were a kid?

- What did you like the most to eat when you were a kid?

- What was one of your best childhood experiences? What made it so special?

- What would your perfect weekend look like?

- Of all the vacations we've had together, what was your favorite and why?

- What's your funniest memory of our dating days?

- Of all the presents you received as a child, which one do you remember the most?

- Our house is on fire, and the kids and I are safe. What five items do you grab before you leave?

- Name three celebrities who you admire. Why do you admire them?

- If you could go back in your life, what would you do differently?

- When were you the most scared in your life?

- What talent do you wish you were better at?

- When were you the happiest in your life?

- What were your biggest fears in school?

- What made you the most proud of yourself?

- When you go to an event or party, what food do you hope will be there?

- What is some of the best advice your parents gave you?

- What's some advice your parents didn't give you, but should have?

- What was your favorite song when you were young?

- What do you wish you could learn?

- What's your favorite part of your graduation/wedding day?

- If you could have a superhero power, what would it be?

- What memory makes you laugh instantly?

- What scares you the most?

- What kind of job would you consider an ideal job? And why?

Even if you think your relationship is kind of boring, these conversations will change your mind. You'll be amazed at the things you didn't know! Think of it as rediscovering your partner. It will make them more interesting, and it will reconnect you. You may learn something about your partner that maybe they haven't shared with anyone until now. It's a gift and should be treated as such. Also, asking these questions will give you tons of ideas for how you can next surprise your spouse. What are you waiting for?

Plan Your Fun

Sometimes, the reality of every day life can cause couples to temporarily lose sight of what brought them together in the first place. It's hard to think of having fun together when you're coming home from work late, taking care of the kids and the house, paying bills, or doing yard work.

Many couples spend too much time with the everyday, more demanding aspects of their relationship, and they forget to have fun and enjoy the more pleasurable aspects of being together. Just letting life go on, and not doing anything about it is not going to do the trick.

What will do the trick? Scheduling a day in the week when you can do something together. It can be something as simple as:

- Watching a movie together
- Having a dinner at home with candles and a bottle of wine
- Just the two of you going for dinner
- Planning an evening at the theatre
- Visiting friends or hosting a party for your old friends

And don't forget to spice it up occasionally! Plan some more rigorous activities that you can both do. They'll make you laugh and feel alive again. Some examples:

- Pillow fighting
- Water pistol fight; clothing optional
- Wrestling in bed
- Tickling
- Roller blading, tennis, golf, or any sport that you can do together

It doesn't have to be physical though to get your blood flowing. For instance:

- Meet at a bar and pretend not to know each other. Then flirt and practice pick up lines. Seduce. Still remember how that goes?
- Cook together.
- Karaoke for two.
- Have a knock-knock joke session.
- Have a bubble bath together.
- Play strip poker.
- Go dancing. If you don't know how to dance, take a class together.
- Have a shower together and wash each other's backs.
- Have sex when your partner least expects it.

If you can afford it, once or twice a year try:

- Taking a couple's mini retreat for a day or two. Go somewhere nice and have fun like you did when you first met. I know a couple who go camping, but you can also take your bikes out for a day trip. Or if you both love antiques, you could make a point of visiting all the quaint shops in your area. Just make sure that whatever activity you choose is something you both love to do.

- Take a short vacation, just the two of you. Rediscover the times when you were alone, with no kids. It might not be possible to do it every year, but plan it in advance and make it happen. It will pay off.

- Combine fun with surprise! Pack your partner's bags, hide them in the car, then suggest going to the mall, but instead, surprise her with a stay at a hotel on the beach.

Get a reliable person to watch your kids while you have your time just for the two of you. If you have to pay for it, do it. Cut expenses somewhere else. It's a good and important investment!

Your kids will be much happier and content if they have
happy parents that love one another,
and enjoy each other's company.
The greatest gift that parents can give to their children is
to let them see how much their parents love each other.

When my wife and I started living together, we had a lot of high-energy fun. We'd chase each other around the house, or hide somewhere and scare the shit out of the other. We'd wrestle in bed a lot, too. But, it's all too easy to forget about these things. We never noticed when we stopped doing these things. It just happened. Like we were finally "grown up." We did grow up, but we also grew apart. Don't let that happen. Having fun together is a sound indicator of how healthy your relationship is. Seriously, do something not so serious. These days we wrestle in bed again. The only difference is now our two sons join in, and then there is one hell of a fight. We love it!

Summary

- Touch and get physical
- Get your blood rushing through your veins
- Schedule time for fun

Exercise

- In addition to the above, list as many face-to-face, high-energy activities you can think of. The sillier and more outrageous the better. Anything that leads to a belly laugh.
- Block some time for your regular fun. It can be fifteen minutes each day, an entire evening on Fridays, or a whole day every now and then.
- Just start doing it.

The Power of Genuine Touch

Cuddling is one of the best ways to show physical affection. Cuddling and touching releases oxytocin, which reduces stress and makes us feel good.

You may not know this, but oxytocin is also released through eating fatty foods. Think about that the next time you finish that second bag of salty crisps! But more importantly, oxytocin controls empathy and emotional response, and it's vital for getting the feelings of closeness and intimacy.

If you haven't been cuddling for some time, and you aren't sure what the best moves are, worry no more! Cuddling is easy and fun.

Cuddling comes in a variety of forms, and not all cuddling means you have to literally lean on each other. Some men freeze when they hear the word cuddling, but it doesn't have to be intimidating.

Cuddling can be:

- Sitting close to each other on the couch
- Holding hands when you walk together
- Giving each other a soft foot or neck massage
- A gentle touch or a kiss will do wonders

These are all signs of genuine, loving feelings that are simple to do.

You don't have to wait for your partner to initiate cuddling. Initiate it yourself. And if you feel like being on the receiving end, just say, "I would really appreciate it if you could (hold me, touch me, hold my hand). It would make me feel so much better."

My wife and I usually cuddle this way after the kids have gone to bed. We'll sit together on the sofa and talk. Sometimes we'll just sit next to each other, I'll hug my wife, and sometimes it's the other way around. Or she might take my head in her lap and give me an eye massage because I asked her. She knows I like it, so she'll do it for me. Or I might rub her feet or give her a head and neck massage after a stressful day at work. Then we'll talk about how our day went. Sometimes it might take just fifteen minutes or so, sometimes it's more. There's no pressure. The best thing about it is that we look forward to it. It's a wonderful way of saying "Hello, how's you day been?" while relaxing. It just feels good.

Summary

- Cuddling releases oxytocin which reduces stress and makes us feel good.
- Cuddling can also be just sitting next to each other, or holding hands while you have a walk.
- If you'd like to be touched, don't be afraid to ask for it.

Shut Up and Listen Good

Being a good listener takes practice and hard work. Being a lousy listener, unfortunately, comes all too easy.

Of course, it's also important to know how to say something mindfully, and I'll cover that right after this section. That said, I believe it's even more important to first learn how to just shut up and listen to your partner.

What Makes a Good Listener

Actively listening, asking questions and showing genuine interest, while seeking to understand what your partner is actually saying, are traits of a good listener. I believe it's one of the most useful skills in communication in general, and will help you immensely in your life, not just in your relationship. I also think you can easily learn it, or get better than you are now.

What makes a good listener stand out?

Encourage

Listening while remaining completely silent feels awkward, and might be perceived as lack of interest. On the other hand, abruptly interrupting makes a poor listener. Where is the fine line? Well, somewhere in the middle, and there are a couple of good practices that you can use.

While your partner talks, nod and encourage them by using phrases like:

- Go on
- I understand
- Interesting
- Tell me more
- I never thought about it that way
- Any combination of above

Beware though, I'm not saying you should fake it. What I'm saying is, while being genuinely interested in what your partner has to say, consciously encourage them to tell you more. It makes your partner feel good (as he sees that you are actively listening), and it gets you more information.

Summarize

Summarize the meaning of what was said.

- Let me see if I've got you. You said …
- So what you are saying is …
- Let me see if I've got you right. What you're saying is that …

- So let me see if I get what you're saying … (then repeat what you heard them say, fully trying to reflect what you believe your partner is feeling, thinking, etc.)

Seek clarification

It's wise to check for more background. Similar to summarizing, it shows your genuine interest and reveals underlying issues, if there are any. To do that, use the five magic questions I'll discuss next, and avoid asking *why* and closed-ended questions. Let's walk through each of those questions.

Use the five magic questions

The five magic questions are "magical" because they lead to the underlying concern surprisingly fast. The five magic questions are in their nature open-ended, and require the other person to explain, as opposed to answering questions that ask for simple yes or no responses.

The five magic questions are:

1. How?
2. What?
3. When?
4. Where?
5. Who?

Examples:

- How come?

- How do you know?

- What do you mean?

- What makes you think that?

- When did this begin?

- Where did it happen?

- Who told you that?

Stop asking WHY

Unless you deliberately want to negate something, or deliberately make your partner stubborn about something, stop asking questions starting with *why*.

- Why didn't you …

- Why did you …

A question that starts with why *will get you a bullshit answer.*

How come?

- The person asked doesn't know or hasn't thought about it.

- The person asked does know, but doesn't want to tell you. Many times, because they expect you might not like what you'll hear, they may modify answers they think you do want to hear, which makes them bullshit answers.

I wouldn't rely on that answer if I were you.

Answering to *why* begets justification with "Because …" Even if you deconstruct the word "justification," you'll find two words: justice and fiction. You get the point?

There is another important aspect to avoiding asking *why* questions. By asking them, it's impossible to discover the underlying issues. Answering with *because* only gets the person more entrenched in their position, and with every additional *why* the person digs deeper and deeper, while you're not getting any new information at all.

Especially if you want to change a behavior of a person you are talking to, never ask why they did or said something, but use the five magic questions! By the way, that holds true also for talking to your children.

Avoid closed-ended questions

Closed-ended questions are questions that can be answered with a simple yes or no. You will solve no conflict by getting just yes or no answers, except if you really didn't have a conflict, or you're a robot.

Asking closed-ended questions is a bad practice because the answers *yes* and *no* contain too little information. In order to understand the conflict and reach a satisfying solution, you need to know more. Simple yes and no answers will not get you there.

Your big but can destroy your relationship

In our society it seems like every other sentence contains the word
but. The other person says something, and we soon follow with a big
but. *But* is a little word with big consequences. It works to delete
everything that your spouse had just said, and sets you pulling against
each other. It builds resentment and is, as such, damaging to your
relationship. Instead of using *but*, just replace it with, "Yes, and …"

The structure is as follows:

"Yes, (find a point that agrees with what was just said), AND (at the
same time)" you state how you stand.

Alternatively use:

"Yes, and at the same time …" or "Yes, and in addition to that …"

Example:

Statement: "A child that age should not have a mobile phone."

"Yes," and response: (1) "he is too young, AND (2) even though he
may easily lose it (3) it would help us know where he is if something
happens".

Saying, "Yes, and …" does NOT mean that you agree with what was
just said. You don't have to. It's not about agreeing or not agreeing.
It's about acknowledging that your partner has just said something
that you might or might not agree with, AND at the same time
expressing your own opinion.

Exercise

- For the next couple of days, pay attention when *but* sneaks into a conversation.
- Start replacing your *buts* with "Yes, and …"

It will feel awkward at first, because we're not used to doing it. But pay attention closely. Your partner will start responding positively to your new way of communication. It will not go unnoticed.

Avoid giving unsolicited advice

Remember, sometimes we don't need a solution. Sometimes we just want someone who we trust and feel secure with (hopefully this is your spouse), to talk about some issue. Maybe it's a problem at work, a dilemma with a friend, a habit you would like to change, or any non-couple dilemma that triggers uncomfortable feelings in you.

Did you ever start to explain something to your spouse, and all of a sudden your spouse interrupts you, and finishes your words and/or starts dispensing advice as if he already knew what you were going to say?

How did you feel? Somehow, spouses always seem to have a ready-to-use recipe at their fingertips, ready to be dispensed in all their wisdom, and magically make all your dilemmas go away-without ever having to listen to what you have to say! I am being sarcastic here, but you get the point.

It seems in our society, we are not taught how to just shut up and listen. We jump to conclusions because we already know! Well, the reality is, we don't. We can't see into other people's minds. And even if we get it right sometimes, we get it wrong as well. In absence of active listening, our conclusions are more likely to be just guesses, not to mention how much we'll annoy the other person.

I remember my father getting mad when my mother interrupted him and "finished his thoughts." Surely, his reaction felt a bit overblown, but in reality, he was just frustrated because my mother didn't have the patience to listen until the end.

That said, it doesn't mean you can't say what's on your mind, especially if you know the solution. What I'm saying is that you listen first, and resist the temptation to dispense "advice" before you have heard the whole story. Then simply ask your spouse if they are interested in hearing what you think about it. If the answer is yes, tell them about it. If not, save it for later. Maybe they aren't in the mood right now to listen to your advice, and just want to be heard.

Giving unsolicited advice is a bad practice because it builds resentment. That holds true especially if this practice becomes a pattern of how you talk to each other. Then you've just got yourself another reason to avoid talking to one another. I'm guessing this is not what you want, and so if you recognize yourself in this, stop doing it. Your spouse will be thankful and you will both start enjoying your conversations more.

Empathize

It's a nice feeling to know that your partner really "feels" you. In other words, you are telling your partner that you can put yourself into their shoes. Many times this is exactly what your partner is looking for, because they already know the solution.

- "I understand how you must be feeling ..."
- "You must have felt ..."

In other words, it's a genuine "poor baby" response. We all need that and it's nothing to be ashamed of, even for men!

Match your partner and become irresistible

After you master your listening skills, you will already be ahead of 95 percent of the population. But if you really want to create a deep sense of profound connection with your partner, try matching.

What is matching?

You surely have noticed two people who get on really well tend to match each other's communication, and non-verbally, as well. What do I mean? Imagine that you don't hear what they say, but you see them. They tend to match their bodies. They talk with a similar tempo, have similar body posture, they even wave with their hands in a similar way. This is called matching, and it's a very well-researched phenomenon of human behavior. You can observe it yourself by paying attention the next time you see people talking who are obviously fond of each other.

It's not hard once you learn it. It just takes a little bit of practice.

Now, I'm not talking about mimicking. If you mirror your spouse's every move, they will soon want to hit you in the face. Matching your partner's body language means subtly and gradually adapting to your partner's way of communication, *including* their body language. What do I mean?

- The tone of your spouse's voice
- The tempo and speed of your spouse's speech
- The posture of his body, like crossing or uncrossing the legs
- Gestures and hand movements
- Breathing

In short, matching isn't something that will influence whether your relationship will work or not, but if you know how to do it, and with a little practice, it will make you irresistible. What's wrong with being irresistible to your spouse?

Be your partner's coach

Sometimes, it will become obvious to you that your partner is stuck and doesn't know what to do. Sometimes it will be related to work, but it can be from any area of life. When this is the case, it's nice to be able to talk to someone who we feel safe with and trust. Hopefully this is also your partner. As I stated before, I have found that in a majority of cases, our partners already know a solution, and just want to be listened to. All that they expect from us is a "poor baby, everything will be fine" soothing. Try this first.

Then again, when your partner does want to hear what you think about a certain issue, maybe they want you to give advice, what do you do? Instead of stating your opinion and dispensing advice, many times it's much more helpful to help your partner find the solution themselves. This is because a solution found this way has more value to your partner than if someone tells them what to do.

Example:

- "What's up baby? You seem tense lately. Do you want to talk about it?"
- "I don't know, I'm just feeling so anxious lately."

Start exploring what's going on by saying:

- "Tell me more about it."

As you know now, we don't consider "*Why* are you anxious?" to be a good question, because it asks for *because*, and you'll get a bullshit answer.

You could ask, "What are you anxious about?" though. But that would be right off the bat.

Rather, try something else. Professional coaches know this, and make a living from asking questions such as:

- How do you feel when you are anxious?
- Where in your body do you have this feeling?
- When did this feeling begin?

- What do you mean by that?

- How do you know?

- What have you thought so far?

- So what do you think you might do?

- How else might you handle it?

- If you did know, what would that be?

- What has worked for you in the past?

- What else?

- Which ones seem most important to you?

- How do you think that will work out?

- So, what stops you?

- Everybody? Always? Never? Nobody? Nothing? All? No one?

- Who says? According to whom?

- Compared to whom? Compared to what?

- What would happen if you did ...? What would happen if you didn't?

- How would you feel if you were in the same situation this time next year?

- Why is that important to you?

- What will you stand to lose if you don't fix it?

Asking this way, you are helping your partner develop possible solutions on their own. This is extremely valuable because it will not be your idea but theirs. As such, it has a greater chance of sticking with them.

By the way, this is what coaching is all about. It's a great gift to be able to ask meaningful questions that make people think and develop their own solutions. I will not go further into this as it's beyond the scope of this book, but just for a taster, after hearing what could be the possible solutions your partner came up with, your next and very powerful questions is, "So, what stops you from doing ...?" and you would take it from there.

It will make your partner think, see things from another perspective and, most important, find their own solution. Your partner will be thankful for that.

Lastly, if your partner doesn't feel like being coached as described above, or has totally run out of ideas and really wants your advice, now's your chance! But be gentle and frame your ideas with "How about if you ...?" Or "Have you thought about ...?" And/or use some humble disclaimers like "It's maybe just me, but ..."

Let me warn you right here, though. Do this only if you are asked. Coaching and family is not something that necessarily goes well together, because you are emotionally connected and this prevents much needed objectivity.

Even though you might find these questions great, don't make them your way of asking things in your daily life. Maybe try once when your partner specifically asks you to tell him what you think, and see how it goes. If it goes well and your partner likes it, you can use them when it's appropriate. Think of them like special tools that you use only now and then, but when you do, they come in super handy.

Summary

Encourage:

- "I understand, go on."
- "Go ahead."
- "Interesting, tell me more."

Summarize:

- Check to make sure you understood the meaning correctly.
- "Let me see if I've got you. You said …?"
- "So what you are saying is …?"
- "Let me see if I got you right. What you're saying is that …?"

Seek clarification:

- Use the magic five questions starting with what, how, where, when and who
- Avoid asking why
- Avoid closed-ended yes or no questions

Get rid of the buts.

Replace *buts* with "Yes, and … " phrases.

Avoid offering advice unless you are asked to. If you already know the solution, resist giving it unless asked. If you are in doubt, ask your spouse. Avoid finishing sentences. Just shut up and listen.

Empathize:

- Put yourself in your partner's shoes.
- "You must be feeling ..."
- "You must have felt ..."
- "Come here, my poor baby," helps more than you think.
- Avoid sounding patronizing.
- "How can I help you?"

Match your spouse's words and body movements:

- Mirror the tone, tempo and speed of your spouse's speech.
- Watch for posture of the body, gestures and hand movements.
- Synchronize breathing.

Be your partner's coach:

- Help your partner find solutions on their own.

•

Talk Each Other Into Feeling Good

When you want to say something, it's bad practice to focus on the other person and start with that.

Talk about yourself

Focusing on the other person invites resentment because *you* sentences lead to criticism and blaming all too quickly. It disconnects both sides immediately, even before the conversation has actually started.

- YOU …
- YOU made me …
- YOUR (behavior…
- YOU are …
- Did YOU …?
- Why didn't YOU …?
- Why can't YOU (ever) …?

Example:

- John: "Jenny, you think you know all these relationship skills without practicing. You need to be practicing more. You'll be surprised how much you don't know."
- Jenny: "Oh, really? You don't know most of these skills either!"

Jenny felt criticized, so she hit back.

The solution is to talk about yourself, and use sentences starting with *I*.

- Wrong: "You were late picking up the kids."
- Right: "I would like to be sure that the kids are picked up on time."
- Wrong: "You are careless with …!"
- Right: "I'm concerned about …"

Talk about how you feel

Instead of starting with the other person in your mind, which will feel like criticizing and blaming, just say what you feel.

- Bad: "You didn't pay the bills again."
- Good: "I feel bad and angry when you miss paying the bills because …"

Yes, many more words are required to send the same message. Yet, criticism and blaming will do so much more damage to your relationship than any greater number of words ever can.

The perils of always and never

Be careful when you hear yourself or someone else using adverbs like always, never, ever, everybody, everyone, nobody, nothing, all (the time), no one.

- You always _____.
- You never _____.
- Can't you ever _____.
- Everything is wrong.
- You do this or that _____ all the time.
- I've tried everything.
- No one ever helps me.
- You will never change.
- When I try to talk to you, you always …

Those phrases are destructive for several reasons.

They are rarely accurate as they are seen only from the one person's perspective. Many times they're gross exaggerations.

They tend to attack personality rather than behavior, which are traits of criticism and blaming.

They offend even the most well-intentioned people who love you, and don't mean you any harm (like your spouse). Instead of changing your partner's behavior, it will drive your partner further away, and make him dig in and continue with the behavior that frustrates you anyway.

Therefore, avoid using generalizations, avoiding criticism and blaming all together, and get more specific by replacing generalization adverbs with some from the list below:

- Last time
- Yesterday
- Last week
- Last couple of times
- Sometimes
- Often
- Many times

Let's look at this simple example:

"I do all the work."

This is outright demotivating. Hearing this effectively means, "you do nothing." Most probably, this is not true. Even if it's close to reality, there surely are some other areas of life where your partner takes on many, if not all necessary efforts on their shoulders. Hearing "I do all the work," with no specifics behind it makes him or her overwhelmed. Such behavior, if it's not talked over, builds resentment. It's exactly the opposite of what the person who is criticizing wants to achieve.

Another example:

Your partner has a habit of forgetting to lock the door during the night.

Don't rattle off: "You always leave the doors unlocked! Are you trying to get us robbed?"

Rather, say something like: "Honey, it scares me when in the morning I find out that you have left the doors unlocked. When you leave the doors unlocked during the night, it makes me feel unsafe in our own house. I would like you to check the doors before you go to bed, will you?"

Be specific as much as you can. Use the examples to help you get more specific. Generalizations lead your partner to an impression that his or her part of the work is not appreciated at all.

That said, be especially vigilant about generalizations in your own head because it's there where they first happen.

We say in our heads something like, "You never _____" hundreds of times before we say it out loud to our partners. By then it's too late. Remember, everything begins with your thoughts, and all the rest is just a consequence of those. When you listen to how you talk to yourself, using generalizations, decide to stop it. Use the exercise below to help you get out of it.

Exercise

Think of the last topic that led to your voice getting louder.

1. Complete the following sentence:

My partner always/never _____ (insert what annoys you)

2. Now try this:

Last time my partner _____ (insert the same annoyance). At the same time it's also true that _____ (insert when your partner handled things differently) _____ (insert what s/he did differently).

Talk about what you want

Instead of saying what you don't want, state your wish politely by saying "I would like you to …"

Don't: "*I don't want* to go to shopping today."

Do: "*I would rather* go to the beach."

Don't: "*You need* to be more responsible about spending money."

Do: "*I would like* to know that we are on track with our savings so we can buy a new house as we agreed."

Many people are not even aware of how frequently they use this kind of talk. They walk around constantly telling people what they don't want, never telling them what they do want, and then complaining about how poor they are because no one understands them. Well, they are right. Therefore, it's much better practice to tell others what you want, so you can start seeking a satisfactory solution immediately.

There are three big advantages of saying what you want:

- You avoid misunderstandings. Talking about what you don't want is the perfect recipe for misunderstandings. Other people can only guess what it is that you want, but because we all have different maps of the world and see things differently, chances of a guess being accurate are very slim. This sucks and it's frustrating for both sides.

- Negative statements (what you don't want) are less effective, because they lead your brain to do exactly what you don't want. In order for your brain to say no to something, your brain must first create an image of the thing you don't want, and then negate it. The problem is that at this point you're already heading in the wrong direction. That's why the sentence "Don't do that," is much less effective than "Stop that!" If you have kids of your own, you know this already.

- Using a negative statement leads to defensiveness and discouragement. Using a positive statement leads to cooperation and enthusiasm.

On that note, if you are planning to quit smoking, the worst thing you can do is to try to resist the urge. If you say to yourself, "Don't smoke cigarettes. Don't want cigarettes. Don't think about cigarettes!" all you will ever think about is cigarettes, cigarettes, cigarettes.

Let me give you another example. Have you ever been on a diet and, while you were going toward the fridge, you were telling yourself, "I should not eat that cake, I really shouldn't." Then your hand somehow gets into the fridge, you actually see it going there, grabs the plate with the cake, takes it out and then you eat it. This is the same principle.

Now that you know this, next time you might say to yourself "I'm resisting the urge to eat that cake because it's good for me. I'll just take a glass of water instead." I will not go further into this as it's beyond the scope of this book, but the key takeaway is that our brains simply aren't designed to deal with negation very well, so avoid it. See? I didn't say *don't* use it, I said *avoid it*.

Things to watch

•   Make sure you don't misuse the phrase "I feel."

For example "I feel (that) *you* ..." is something you will not have success with. In another words, this is badly disguised blaming and accusation that will not bring success.

Wrong: "I feel that you are irresponsible, because you didn't pay the bills again."

Right: "I feel bad and angry when you miss the deadline for paying the bills, because ..."

- Make sure you don't misuse "I would like you _____."

"I would like *you* to pick up the kids," is still assertive and starts with *you,* and you are telling your spouse what to do.

"I would like to be sure that the kids are picked up on time," is much better.

- Make sure you don't use the word *we* as a poorly disguised *you.*

Wrong: "We need to stop fighting."

Right: "I feel bad and angry at myself after we fight. I've been thinking, and I have some ideas about what I can do on my part to stop us fighting. I am interested in your opinion."

But I can't talk like this, it's not natural!

You might think it's hard to start talking like this. That it's not natural. That's because you are not used to doing it. You might say that it feels fake. Yes, it feels fake because you are not used to it. Then again, what is so wrong with being nice and considerate when you talk? If necessary, fake it until you make it.

Don't let all this overwhelm you. What's the hurry anyway? Take one language pattern at a time and start practicing. Start, for example, with avoiding generalizations (always, never, nothing). Next, focus on talking about what you want (and not what you don't want). And so on.

With practice the language patterns as discussed will become natural to you, and you will be amazed how much negative energy has disappeared. Remember, the higher goal is not to let little every day issues grow into big problems that, down the road, will damage your relationship and your marriage. Applying the concept of how to talk mindfully, you can solve most of the every day issues in a non-threatening way, while inviting insight, cooperation and understanding.

And, persist. Remember, it's not about the examples word-by-word, but the principles used behind those examples. Use them just as a starting point and then figure out your own "language." Couple this with a friendly tone of yours, and a show of genuine care, and you are golden and well on your way to a successful and productive conversation.

Exercise

- Take a piece of paper and divide it into two columns. Name the left column "before" and right column "now."

- In the left column, write 10 sentences beginning with the word *you* and any generalizations that you often use when talking to your spouse.

- Then use the right column to write down more appropriate statements by using one or more of the above described principles of mindful talking.

- Read both versions out loud. If those sentences were directed at you, which version would you prefer?

Have a Feel Good
No Big Deal Conflict

We tend to look at conflict as a big, hairy beast that's going to eat us alive. Things get unpleasant, and there will always be something that you are not so pleased with.

Yet, conflicts don't have to necessarily be bad. Conflicts are okay! In fact, it's how we look at them. If your relationship is alive and kicking, you have conflicts. You have disagreements and it's a given.

What's important is how you react to the conflicts. It's about your response. It's not about the fight, but how you fight. It's how you express your disagreement in a structured and non-threatening way. And by doing so, you have a much higher chance of getting your message across, while not harming the relationship, and making it even stronger.

In this section you will learn how to:

- How to approach to your spouse mindfully
- Receive complaints and criticism gracefully
- Prevent meltdowns when things start getting out of control

- Go for a win-win solution
- Apologize mindfully

By following those steps, you will have a real chance to discover that you can in fact have a conflict without your heart beating like hell, your face turning red, your hands sweating, steam pouring out of your ears and requiring half an hour just to calm down.

How to Approach to Your Spouse Mindfully

At this point, I want you to remember how we addressed the difference between how we treat our valuable customers and how we treat our own spouses.

Even if you are annoyed with your customer, do you just pick up the phone and start yelling at them? I suppose not. You would probably first ask them how they've been, maybe you would mention something nice, and remember something about the last time you heard from them, or maybe ask about their kids.

Then you would probably use some disclaimer like, "Listen, maybe it's not a big deal, but I really want to mention that I highly value our relationship ..."

You would probably be mindful of how you would phrase your words. You wouldn't sugarcoat an unpleasant situation, but you would still take their feelings into account before opening your mouth.

That is what we are aiming for here.

That said, make no mistake. I am not telling you now, or anywhere else in this book, that you should be sugarcoating difficult or unpleasant situations with your spouse, and thus become more of an actor than a partner in flesh and blood.

What I'm saying is that it's simply not fair to give your spouse any less of a nice treatment than you would to your most valuable customer (who, by the way, doesn't share the same bed with you). Lastly, it doesn't need to be a customer. Another example is your best friend, or anyone else outside your family who you deeply care for.

So, how do you approach to your spouse mindfully?

Start slow

- Make sure you are relaxed, or at least in a neutral state. Do not start your conversation if you or your partner is in a bad state.
- Say something nice first.
- Thank or praise your spouse for something from today or the week. Mean it.

Use humble disclaimers

Use humble disclaimers as soft openers. Only when you both feel safe and connected can a productive conversation take place, and a solution be found. In this section I want to share with you how you can further soften your statements. It's by using humble disclaimers in a Lt. Columbo style.

For the uninitiated, Lt. Columbo was a television character, played by Peter Falk successfully for three decades. Columbo was a detective in the Los Angeles Police Homicide Bureau. He was exceptionally successful at solving crimes because he managed to put people at ease, allowing them to open up and tell him things. He was using humble disclaimers like these:

- It's probably just me, but ...
- I'm probably thinking about this all wrong, but ...
- You've probably thought about this already, but ...
- I wish I knew, but I just don't know how to handle this ...
- I'm not sure if this is on point, but ...
- I don't know exactly how to say this, and I hope you'll help me, but ...
- I'm not sure if it's okay me bringing this up, but ...
- I hope you'll forgive me for not knowing quite how to say this, but ...

The power of humble disclaimers is not in diminishing your point to get more likeable, or anything like that. It's in sending the message that you are accepting the possibility that things said are only your perception of things. You are effectively saying, "I might be wrong, and I am ready to listen to your point as well."

Again, pay attention here. I am not saying you should act submissive or anything like that. I am just saying that sometimes it's appropriate to further soften up your statements to establish an early connection between the two of you, to make it easier for your partner to really listen. Which is what you want, right?

Also, maybe it seems to you that the sentences listed above contradict the rule of not using *buts*, and replacing them with "Yes, and ..." They are not, because in all those cases, *but* plays an important role in deliberately negating the first part of the sentence, while achieving its goal—let the other person open up more easily.

Address the elephant in the room

Sometimes it's hard for a spouse to raise an issue as they expect opposition, or is in fear of a fight. But we all feel it. Something is in the air. You feel the tension. But things don't get said. Lead the way and address the issue yourself! Address the obvious.

- "I feel the tension (you're angry with me). Can you help me understand the reason?"

A good approach, almost sure-fire, to soften your message further down the road is to use some of Lt. Columbo's humble disclaimers.

- "Maybe it's just me, but I feel the tension (you're angry with me). Can you help me understand the reason?"

Avoid asking *why,* for example, "Why are you angry?" because, as previously explained, it makes the other person more entrenched.

They will find all kinds of reasons to answer your *why* that may or may not be true.

You can also literally name the "elephant" and start on a funnier note by saying something like this:

- "Hey, I feel there is an elephant sitting on this couch right next to us and it's getting a bit uncomfortable." Then continue, "Maybe it's just me, but I feel something is wrong. Can you help me understand what it is?" While talking, touch your partner's hand gently and smile.

The point is that you state the obvious. You state that something is wrong, and ask for confirmation if that is how your partner feels as well. Your partner will thank you, and respect you for your courage and willingness to talk calmly about something that obviously they are bothered by as well.

If you find the issue a tough nut to break, I strongly suggest you both agree to put it off, and then try again some time later. I'll discuss that in detail in a dedicated section later on, so stay tuned.

If even after talking about the issue again, you find that the issue still triggers strong negative emotions, and then it might be appropriate to resort to intentional dialogue, which I will explain in detail in the continuation of this book.

Be specific

After a soft start, it's good practice to be as specific as you can about what bothers you. This way you avoid criticism and blaming automatically. Secondly, by being specific, it makes it easier for your partner to relate to a specific event or series of events in the past, pay closer attention next time, and adjust behavior in the future.

One way of doing that is by using phrases that contain *when you* and combine them with stating how you *feel* about it.

"*When you* do _____ I feel like _____." Or "I feel _____ *when you* _____."

Example:

Bad: "You are always late!"

Good: "When you are late without giving me any advance notice, I feel taken for granted."

Notice there is the word *you* in the sentence, but the emphasis is on your feelings.

If you get overwhelmed

Reading this, you may have gotten overwhelmed. You may have the impression that you're more likely to get a license to fly a spacecraft than learn how to approach to your spouse mindfully.

For example, the next time you want to express your disagreement, just remember to use one of the openers and soften up your start a little bit. See how it goes. If it works, remember it and take it from there. Next time start paying attention to *you* phrases, and start replacing them with *I feel* and then take it from there. You get the point.

Remember, there is no contest, and there is no winner or loser, but you can both win or lose, depending on what you do and how consistently you apply what you've learned.

Exercise

- Think about the last time you complained to your spouse.
- Think of how you would do it now.
- Would there be a difference in how your complaint was received by your spouse, and what results would you achieve?

Exercise

- Think about the last time there was unspoken tension between both of you that you didn't address.
- Think of how you would address the issue softly and lead the conversation further, by following the principles you've learned.
- Commit to trying this the next time you feel tension between you. Show up confident in your new abilities, and address the issue.

Summary

- Don't start when you are stressed or angry. Calm down first. If possible, use a dedicated time to deal with stuff that bothers you.

- Start slow. Praise. Thank your partner for something first.

- Soften up your opening by using a humble disclaimer.

- Address the issue and be specific.

- Use the principles of how to shut up and listen, and how to talk mindfully, and then seek a win/win as you'll learn shortly.

How to Receive Criticism Gracefully

This section is about how to react if you are on the receiving end; if you are the target of the complaining.

We covered how to approach to your spouse mindfully, but it might be that your partner is still resorting to the old habits, or is not yet aware of the new skills you have. You might have already stopped criticizing yourself, but your partner is still criticizing you. What to do?

Especially if you are a target of criticism, you feel threatened. Your brain, specifically your amygdala, perceives the situation as danger. Your blood flushes to your face and your heart starts beating. If you let your amygdala take over control, you know what's going to happen. We don't want that, so you have to learn to act differently. How?

Step 1. Resist the temptation to strike back

Breathe and resist striking back.

Remind yourself that criticism is a defensive reaction of your partner to something that they perceive as danger. You might not (yet) know what that is, but that doesn't mean you should strike back and engage in a fight. That would be repeating the same mistakes from the past, and you don't want that.

Also, sometimes you'll be literally taken off guard. You will not know what to say and how to respond so as not to make things worse. These are some proven ways of how to react that always work:

Step 2. Accept gracefully

- "I am sorry to hear that."
- "I haven't thought of things that way."

Or:

If you have a hard time accepting the criticism gracefully, state the obvious:

- "I feel criticized now. Can you help me understand?"

This way you have just bought yourself additional time. When your partner starts explaining to you things, and you hear something that you disagree with, resist the temptation to interrupt, and do the opposite—encourage your partner to go on. It will have a very calming effect on both of you. But don't stop there.

Step 3. Listen carefully

In light of receiving criticism well, your newly acquired listening skills will come extremely handy.

While listening, encourage your partner to go on and tell you the whole story with: "I'm listening, go on," "Go ahead," "I understand," "Tell me more," and other phrases that were covered earlier. Summarize and then seek clarification by using the five magic questions while avoiding asking *why* and closed-ended questions. Avoid using *buts*. Show empathy.

Step 4. Dig deeper politely

We tend to assume that we know what the other person is thinking. But in reality, we are guessing. Ask questions like:

- What do you mean?
- Can you help me understand?

You will be amazed how many times you'll hear something that will not correspond to what you originally thought.

Remember, if you're being criticized, most probably there is a belief behind it that is "feeding the criticism." If you want to overcome the issue, you may want to try to discover what's actually going on by asking questions like:

- How do you know?
- Address generalizations by asking: Everybody? Always? Never? Nobody? Nothing? All? No one?

- Who says? According to whom?

- Compared to whom? Compared to what?

Beware of sounding patronizing or sarcastic though, and watch your tone.

Step 5. Seek resolution

- Ask "How can I help?" or "What would you want me to do?"

If that is something you can easily agree to, go for it. There is no need for lengthy discussions if that is so. If not, find a solution using a win-win approach that we will cover shortly.

Step 6. Thank your spouse for bringing the issue up

Don't forget to thank your spouse for bringing the issue up! It's encouragement for your spouse not to feel threatened, and to tell you about stuff next time, as well. Even though you might not agree with what was just said, you do want to have the communication channel open also in the future. The real trouble starts when there is no communication.

Finally, if at any stage you feel that it's not going to work, and the conversation just makes you more angry by the second, absolutely resort to suggestions from the next section that covers occasions when things are starting to get out of control.

Summary

- Accept criticism gracefully. Remember, even though it's aimed at you, criticism is a defensive reaction of your partner to something they perceive as danger.

- Buy some more time and seek for more information.

- Use your best listening skills.

- If there is something that you can do, do it right away. If not, try seeking a win-win solution. Thank your partner. It's how you motivate him or her to talk to you next time, as you want to have the communication channels open.

Exercise

- Think of the last time your spouse was complaining and possibly criticizing you.

- Close your eyes, and think how you could have reacted differently, following the principles covered in this section.

- Commit to trying this the next time you feel you are being criticized.

How to Prevent a Meltdown

Identifying when you are getting angry and managing it, is a skill you want to master. It's your calm down hotline that will prevent you from saying and doing things that you'll later regret.

Understanding your anger

What I'm going to talk about here is something that will happen much more often than you wish. To bring our amygdala, part of the brain responsible for fight or flight response, under conscious control takes some practice, but the rewards are great.

To my assessment, this skill alone is (almost) a marriage savior per se, because it limits the number of really bad, unreasonable, nasty experiences that you have with one another.

I am talking about a skill for becoming aware of your growing anger, and managing the conversation that follows, while this is still possible and with no harm done.

It's like you want to talk with your spouse in the middle of a tornado. Debris is flying around, you are shouting, your spouse is shouting, the wind is roaring, you can't even hear each other, huge noises all around ... . You get the picture. Nice setting to have a talk, right?

Now imagine this. You get yourself out of the way of the tornado and simply wait for it to pass. Then, you come back, invite your spouse to sit together on the porch, have a drink and talk. Which way would you prefer? I mean, if you're not an obsessive marriage adrenaline junkie, the answer is clear. So, which way do you want it to be?

Saying that, it doesn't mean you should be ignoring an issue. Not at all. You should talk about it, but only if you are both calm when you do. That's the whole point. You want to avoid getting to a point when things get nasty, feelings get hurt and people really get angry.

Research shows that couples who are skilled at stopping escalation of a tension during a discussion, before things get out of control, are the ones that thrive in the long run. Because nasty fights are just that-nasty. They build resentment and negative thoughts. Anger invites anger.

All said, you will sometimes still screw up things, and let your anger take over. It's interesting, but we usually know when we are screwing things up as we are doing it, yet somehow we still do it. We are all human beings, and that is okay as long as it's a rare exception and not a rule. Sadly, many couples do exactly the opposite. They let things get overheated for almost anything, as a rule and not an exception. This is a call for trouble.

What you're about to learn here is a skill that takes you in the opposite direction. You'll learn how to identify when you are approaching the "danger zone" before you are even there, and what you can do the next time, when there is still time and with no harm done.

When emotions run hot, it's important how you react. If your heart is already pumping like crazy at 150 beats per minute, you won't be able to hear anything that your spouse is saying, no matter how hard your spouse tries. Your amygdala has taken over full control and you are now officially in emergency mode. Your body starts to produce vast quantities of adrenaline, which triggers the fight or flight response, the same as it had a thousand years ago when your ancestor met a beast in the woods and had to decide whether to fight, hide in the bushes or get the hell out of there as soon as possible.

Looking for clues that steam is building up

How can you recognize when things are getting a bit overheated?

As you now know, when we are in danger (literal or perceived), our defense mechanisms kick in. You know you are there because:

- Your heart starts pumping
- Your feel a rush of blood to your face
- Your face gets reddish and warmer
- You feel spinning in your chests or in your stomach
- Some people report a growing pressure in their chests
- You start breathing more quickly
- Your hands may start sweating

Why is letting anger off so damaging?

First of all, it's because you can't really discuss anything anymore. If you let things get out of control, you will be in the position where you no longer hear what your partner is saying, as if you are completely deaf. You are now thinking more about how to save your self-esteem than about the topic.

If things get out of control frequently, a less talked about, but not any less damaging, phenomenon happens. Your brain starts to associate your partner with danger, the same as our ancestor associated a tiger with danger. Once this association is established, even the most well-intentioned behavior of your partner is accompanied with suspicion and disbelief, the same as you would closely monitor a tiger lurking around even if he is not hungry.

There is another aspect of letting things get out of control frequently. More often than not, kids are watching. If they watch this happening too often, they unconsciously form the same pattern themselves. Aside from our genuine love and care, is there any greater gift then equipping our kids with productive behavior patterns so they can engage in their own relationships with confidence, and have a happy and healthy relationship themselves?

What to do when you realize the steam is building up?

When things are starting to get out of control, and you are getting angry, your immediate goal is to stop the conversation mindfully. The next step is to reclaim control of your brain. You do so by using the pause to calm down and leave the fight or flight emergency mode. After you've successfully calmed down, you can continue the conversation, and find a solution that fits the purpose.

Note that I didn't say you should not talk about the issue or avoid it. I said that when things are getting out of control, and your amygdala is starting to take over the controls of your brain, you have to stop and pause before continuing.

Let's have a look at a couple of proven techniques for each of the three steps.

Stop the conversation mindfully

Find below a collection of sample stop sentences:

- "I need to calm down, would you give me a minute?"
- "Let's take a break, I need to calm down."
- "I feel tension between us and I don't want us to start arguing. Let me think about it and let's talk again some time later. Is (propose the time) good for you or would you prefer some other time?"
- "I feel (upset, offended, sad) now."
- "I don't think this is going in the right direction. Let's talk about it later. What about when the kids go to bed?"
- "I would like us to continue this conversation, but I need to calm down as right now I am starting to get upset. Can we do it this evening or maybe tomorrow evening?"
- "Can we take a break? I'm starting to get upset now?"
- "Honey, I'm sorry but I'm getting far more upset than I would like. I think it will be better for both of us if we continue this conversation some time later. What about tomorrow morning, while we take a walk together?"
- "I hear what you're saying, and it's not that I want to run away, but I'm getting upset now. Can we do it later?"
- "It's not you, it's me."

Make sure you don't sound arrogant, patronizing or something in-between. Just sound as sincere as you can, look your partner in the eyes and try to soften your tone. Maybe do a rehearsal a couple of times before. Yes, it takes some effort, but it pays off immensely.

After saying this, beware! No further arguing, no comments, even half loud. And, no door slamming.

Politely resist the temptation of your spouse trying to suck you back into an already heated conversation. Explain calmly why you are pausing, and assure your partner you WILL come back and not forget it. Better so, ask if it's okay with them. We all want to solve our problems fast and, especially until you are used to this process, for your partner, your withdrawal might be misunderstood as fleeing.

My wife and I use the phrase "My amygdala is vibrating right now." That means to both of us that from now on we are entering the danger zone of the other. The word "amygdala" is unusual enough so it gets heard even in the heat of the moment. Usually that's more than enough to cool things off so we can start differently.

Sometimes one of us says, "Hey, it's not you, it's me. It's (then explain feelings and concerns)." This always works.

We also know each well enough to recognize small changes on the face, and by observation of each other's body language, that something isn't quite right. My wife would, for example, ask me, "Did I step onto something here?" I would kind of smile and admit, "Yeah, as a matter of fact you did," and then I would explain how I feel and why.

Calm down

Now that you have got some time, spend it wisely. For example, steaming somewhere and saying, "What a nasty pig he is, leaving socks all over the place," is only going to add salt to the wound. Don't fall into the trap of stewing in negative thoughts because this will only increase your anger.

When someone says, just relax, it's usually easier said then done, especially in the heat of the moment, right? Still, there are some proven ways and techniques that are not hard to learn, that relax you brain very effectively without deliberately "relaxing." It's all connected to how our brain works. Let me explain a couple of ways to do it. We have briefly touched the most important already—moving your body.

Move your body

The most effective way to relax is by moving your body. I mean literally moving your legs and arms and doing something with them, not moving your fingers over a keyboard or a remote control.

You can't think straight about something when you're jumping and running around and your heart is beating at 150 beats per minute. This is the reason to go jogging instead of simply walking, even though walking is way better than sitting at home and watching TV or checking emails.

Why is moving your body so important? It's because when we exercise, our brain releases endorphins. By the way, did you know that endorphins are also released during laughter, eating chocolate and having sex? Because of this chemical phenomenon, it's wrong to be looking for a solution to a problem while feeling bad or angry. On the contrary, you first have to feel good, and then look for a solution. Moving your body and exercising raises the level of endorphins in your brain, which in turn makes you feel good. So there you have it.

Go to the gym, go running or simply have a walk. It's known that the muscles in your legs consume the most energy, and this is what you want right now. You want your body to think something else, which is how to move. If you are not into walking, mow the lawn and be useful. Speaking of useful, you can start putting dishes in the dish washing machine, taking the laundry out, repairing a garage door, or going out and throwing a ball with the kids. Maybe this would be a good time to finally beat the dust out of the rugs.

It can also be as simple as saying "I need to get a glass of water. Want some as well?" This gesture of yours serves two purposes. The first one is that it gets you on your feet and get you walking. Secondly, it shows your partner that you care for them, even though you are having a disagreement.

Anything that makes your body move will serve the purpose.

I wouldn't suggest going shopping to calm down, at least not every time, if you don't want to anchor yourself into spending money every time you need to calm down. Because if you do that on a consistent basis, your brain will make the connection: angry-shopping-buying nice things for me-pleasure-let's get angry some more!

Further tricks to calm down fast

There are numerous techniques on how to calm down and relax, and whole books are being written just about relaxation. This is not the intention of this book, but at this point, I can recommend something that always works for me.

Excuse yourself mindfully and go to the toilet. This will get you up on your feet. When there, wash your face and hands with cold water. The cold water and washing will help you refocus and calm down. Take a deep breath. Take the air in with your whole body, not just with your chest. Watch your stomach moving up while the air goes in, then you know you're doing it right. Hold your breath for 10 seconds, and then let it out while silently saying "aaaaaaaaaaaaaaaahhhhhh" with a voice going downwards. Repeat at least two times. What you are looking for is a vibrating sensation inside your body as you are saying it. It can be silent so that only you can hear it, because the trick is in the vibration in your stomach, not in the sound itself.

This is a great way to release stress, and useful in all kinds of everyday situations, be it at home or at work.

Change the place of conversation all together

Another way is to change your angle. By changing your angle in a physical space, you will change your point of view and get another perspective.

If you were sitting on a couch, move to a chair. If you were sitting, stand up and move your position. If you were standing, take a seat. If you were in one part of the room, continue the talk at the other side of the room. If your disagreements started in the kitchen, go to the living room.

Better so, go for a walk outside and enjoy the additional benefits of some fresh air.

There is one little known fact that speakers, and people who make a living teaching and giving presentations, publicly know. It's about how to handle situations when people in the audience are giving them a hard time with negative and toxic comments that just won't end. Smart presenters and speakers know that they have to make sure those people change an angle as soon as possible. So they declare a short break, and figure out a reason why people should move around a bit, and change seats. They make sure that the annoying person sits in the opposite side of the room now. Once this person changes the angle physically, it's astonishing how quickly the very same person becomes much more friendly toward the presenter, even though the topic or the way in which the material is presented, hasn't changed.

Changing an angle of view in a physical space changes the angle of view in the mind.

This comes in extremely handy in all kinds of stressful situations, not just at home, but also at work.

Avoid negative self-talk

I understand, it's easier said than done, yet it's crucial. If you use the time in the pause of your conversation to further nurture your bad thoughts, you will come back even more upset than before! Therefore, resist the temptation and distract yourself with something else.

Distract your mind for at least half an hour

If you remember the part of the book where we covered the basics on how our brain works, I said that after the amygdala was set off, our brain needed a "reset" so we can start thinking clearly again (our conscious mind steps in).

Our brains need some time to do that. It has been scientifically proven that men need even more time than women.

You can speed things up by distracting your brain, and doing something completely different for at least half an hour, but that is a minimum for good results.

Don't push for an immediate solution

There is no rule saying that you have to solve problems right away. Instead, take some time.

I am sure you have said that it's best to solve conflicts as soon as possible. I agree.

But I also think that nothing much will happen if we politely take the time to think about it, and get some perspective, especially if things get a little bit overheated. People say that you shouldn't go to bed before resolving conflicts, as I've mentioned before. I think this is really bad advice. That is exactly what you should do! You should in fact sleep on it because in the morning, you will almost surely not feel so strongly about it anymore. New thoughts and new possibilities will be able to emerge and that is what we are looking for.

Allow your subconscious to find a solution. Allow your subconscious to see and examine different points of view. For that, we just need some time. Who knows, maybe in the process you will get a great idea for a win-win scenario.

Don't push too hard for an immediate solution, except if you are hanging on a tree above a bunch of hungry crocodiles.

By politely taking some time to solve your disagreements, you are doing a big favor to yourself and your marriage.

A little fun is not prohibited

Another way to release serotonin and endorphins is to suddenly ask something so unrelated and ridiculous that you both can't help but start laughing. Or put a funny face on and show your partner your tongue. Yes, I know, it's silly, but that's exactly the point! What happens is, during laughter, endorphins are being released in vast quantities. Endorphins, as we already know, make you feel good, same as chocolate and sex. So endorphins are your ally. Smiling wakes them up. Not only will both of you feel good instantly, but you will also send a message to your partner that you don't take yourself so seriously, and sends a "Let's reconnect and repair the damage" message.

Warning! Don't try that if you almost hate each other. It's risky, as it might be interpreted as lack of respect for the feelings of your partner, and you can actually make things worse.

A little secret

Maybe you are not keen on saying something stupid to make you both feel good. That's okay. It's hard sometimes to think of something stupid when you are in the middle of a heated debate. But you can do something else that will do the trick just the same. Go to the toilet or some place no one can see you, and put your finger between your teeth, then hold it there for ten seconds. Notice, you are smiling. But don't worry, I am not going to tell you that you should come back with a fake smile on your face. What happens when you put a finger between your teeth and hold it there for some time? The not-so-well-known fact is that the center of your brain that controls the facial muscles that make your smile happen is coincidentally (or not!) neighboring the very part of the brain that is also responsible for production of serotonin. Serotonin controls sleep, memory, learning, temperature and—you guessed it—mood and behavior.

That is why they say people who smile a lot are happier. Something else is also true. By smiling, even fake smiling, you can make yourself feel good for no reason at all. Sure, at first it will be a fake smile, but after a while you will start to genuinely feel better. It's how our brain works.

Come back and talk again

Now that you are both calm, you can talk again. Make sure you follow the guidelines for how to approach to your spouse mindfully as we discussed earlier.

Write down successes

Noticing a growing anger when there is still time, stopping things going downwards, and turning them back into a pleasant and calm solution-finding talk is a true achievement. Celebrate this small victory. Write it down in a journal and reflect on it each time you do it, because your subconscious will remember it as well, and you'll have an easier time repeating this in the future.

Play to Win and You Will Lose

It's often said that marriage is about sacrifice and compromise. That doesn't sound so great, does it? The reality is though, that in much of your marriage, you will be in constant agreement to do something, this or the other way, with thousands of degrees of grey in-between. This can be anything from picking where to go out for dinner to where you will go on vacation this year, and similar or more serious and far reaching decisions, like the decision to move because your partner got a promotion on the other side of the country, and you have to leave your friends and family behind.

Agreeing to do something done properly can enhance a feeling of connection and harmony, while the opposite leads to frustration, anger, depression and all sorts of negative behaviors.

The wrong way

Couples consciously or unconsciously develop their unique conflict resolution patterns. They may fight for a while and then drop the issue all together. They may decide in favor of the partner who insists most, or is most aggressive or verbally skilled. Or they may take turns with who gets their way, and even keep score on whose "turn" it is to get his way. Or both partners compromise by giving up some of what they want, with no one getting what they want.

Years down the road, sometimes decades, the only thing that is left is a feeling of total emptiness. The only thing that is left is a feeling that they never had a chance to really do what they wanted. It's easy to start hating your partner this way. Commonly, couples get trapped in one of the following unproductive conflict resolution patterns:

- Fight (and win)! In order for one to win, the other has to lose. It's about getting what they want, while not paying attention to the other partner's needs. The "losing party" feels angry, resentful and depressed.

- Flight (and avoid). Main motivation is avoidance of a fight and distraction with something else. It results in all kinds of other excessive and addictive behaviors such as drinking and alcohol abuse, but also more "socially acceptable" behaviors, such as eating disorders, excessive TV, staying late at work, pursuing a hobby excessively at the expense of family time, and an array of other so-called exits.

- Don't get resolved, tension and chronic indecision, leading to chronic anxiety.

- Give-in (give up, submit). Main motivation is to sustain the relationship and be nice. One partner feels weaker than the other and acts so. Such a pattern is commonly accompanied with low self-esteem of a particular partner. It leads to depression.

These behavior patterns lead to negative feelings accumulating over long periods of time. That is why they are especially toxic.

The better way, the win-win approach

Luckily, it doesn't have to be this way as there is a solution.

The win-win approach I am about to teach you is straightforward and can be used for little decisions, such as what to eat or what movie to rent, or more important ones such as what kind of house to buy. The added bonus is that the more you practice it with the small stuff, the easier it gets with the big issues like children, finances, what kind of house to buy or what job to accept. In the end, you will be able to come to solutions that meet the needs and desires of both of you in a satisfying way.

Use the win-win approach any time that:

- You need to decide what you will do about something.
- One of you wants one thing and the other wants something else.

As you will see, it's nothing drastically new, mostly common sense. Also, all those things have been covered in previous sections where we talked about how to listen and talk mindfully.

It's the combination of those skills that makes it effective. The win-win approach has three simple steps:

1. Say what you want

State what you want in a considerate and polite way by using already known phrases like, "I would like to ..."

Really pay attention to avoid talking about what you don't want.

- Less effective: "I don't want to stay at home this evening," is less effective than,

- Much better: "I'd like us to go out and have some fun together."

2. Explore concerns of the other

This step is the most important one. At this step you want to clarify your thoughts and your spouse's, and the preferences that are driving the initially stated wish of both of you. Use the five magic questions and ask:

- "What do you mean?"
- "Help me understand."
- "What you're saying is that ...?"
- "What makes it so important to you?"

Avoid asking why, because as we know it makes the other person only more entrenched in their initial position.

3. Create a solution

Using the details gathered during the exploration phase, you got some clues as to what to propose. Be creative.

Obviously if you came so far, you must feel strongly about the topic. Don't just back off now or comply because you will compromise the whole process when the next similar conflict occurs.

To illustrate what I mean, let's go through an example below. Follow closely the process through all three steps. Again, there are thousands of ways you can do this. What's important is to remember the concept, and to use it the next time an opportunity comes along.

Example: Jeff and Kathy preparing dinner.

Step 1. Say what you want

Kathy: "Let's go somewhere out to eat today, what do you think? "

Jeff: "Hmm. What if we stay at home and have dinner together? Just the two of us."

Step 2. Explore concerns

Kathy: "Well, to be honest, it's not like I don't want to cook, you know how much I enjoy cooking. It's just that the last two weeks have been so busy for both of us, and I feel bad about us not taking any time just for the two of us. Besides, when I walked by the Thai restaurant yesterday I remembered what a great time we had there the last time. Remember how we talked and laughed until they almost kicked us out? I guess, besides the food that was fabulous, I miss that feeling of us going out and having some fun again."

Jeff: "*Yes*, and I've enjoyed that time as well. I can still remember the Mai Thai cocktails we had, and it was nice seeing you laughing all that evening. Well, it makes sense what you're saying, especially because I miss us having fun as well. It's just that lately I've been away from home so much and on business trips, you know, eating at airport restaurants and stuff. It's just that I really wanted to relax a bit, and I had this picture in my mind of us having dinner together at home, talking and just having a good time. You know ... nothing fancy, even though it's just burgers. Then we could talk with the kids about what we want to do this weekend. It reminds me of my childhood when I enjoyed Friday night dinners, because that was when we were making great plans on how we would spend the weekend as a family."

Step 3. Seek a win-win solution

Kathy: "I am thinking ... You know, I have a bad feeling putting on the table *just* burgers, but I am really not into preparing a dinner tonight. Thinking out loud, what if we order some good Thai food that we all love, the kids love it as well, and we can have the dinner at home? We can discuss what we're going to do over the weekend. By the way, I have to tell you about a great idea. Then we could call Nancy to watch the kids, and the two of us could go for a nice Mai Thai cocktail at the Riverbank Lounge. We could listen to some music, watch the sunset at the riverside, comment on people going by, and have some time together. What do you say?"

Jeff: "That sounds like a good idea!"

It's actually what happened to me just the other day. I wanted us to go out and have dinner with friends. My wife didn't. She wanted to spend an evening just with me. I said, "Let's have a dinner together with the kids at home, and then if we still feel like it, let's go just the two of us for a drink to a nearby restaurant that we both love." And we did. My wife wanted some time for just the two of us, and I wanted us to have some fun out. We both got what we wanted.

It's not possible for me to give you an exact recipe for how to find a solution. But from my own experience, thinking for the benefit of both of you and actively wanting to please both of you is half of the job. The second half is to explore what it is that each of you really wants and then, most of the time, the solution falls in your hands if you are the least bit creative.

What to do in especially difficult situations?

There will be cases when it will look like "one way or the other." Typical cases are moving somewhere, or accepting a job hundreds of miles away. Those are not easy decisions. In light of this, sometimes it might be easier to just comply with your spouse, and deliberately disregard your own concerns. It's as bad as forcing a decision your way. If you comply and give-in and pay no attention to your own concerns, then you are a martyr or pretend to be one. Martyrs always die, that's why they are called martyrs. We don't want that.

What can you do?

- Slow down.
- Take time to really dig out all the concerns.
- Be specific. You can't be specific enough. Specifics will give you clues for a solution.
- State your thoughts loudly. There is no place for hidden thoughts when you seek a solution together. If you're afraid you'll hurt your partner's feelings, add a humble disclaimer. Remember, this is NOT the place to hide your thoughts.
- Encourage each other. "Go on," "I am listening," "Tell me more."

- Summarize frequently, so you both know that you understand each other. "Let me see if I got you right ... " Take turns.

- If needed, go back a step or two.

- What you want is as much clarity to what you both want. This is defined by underlying concerns, and that's more than one can understand simply by listening to your opening wish.

- Sometimes, a solution will not be immediately evident, and it might even seem impossible. Take some additional time. Sleep on it. If it's something that will have an impact on your lives for a long time, think what would another day or two, or even a week mean in comparison to the years that follow. Will you want to live with a solution where one feels left out?

- Think in terms of solution sets. Rather than one solution, develop more of them. It's where you follow to satisfy the core needs of each other, while being creative and thinking of several ways of how to satisfy them, like in the example discussed previously. We all like to have a choice. Therefore being able to pick between A and B is much better than if we are offered only A, even though A is already well thought of. This is how our brain works, so keep that in mind.

- When you have the solution on the table, a lot might have been said. Yet, look for clues to see if something has slipped through. Maybe one was afraid to (re)open something, knowing that it might change everything. Take that risk and ask.

- Look for clues for anything that still feels unfinished. If you feel there is something left unspoken, address it. Remember when we were talking about addressing the elephant in the room? Use that principle now.

- Pay attention to how you feel about what you have just agreed upon. Are you excited about the solution or have mixed feelings? Anything you have on your mind and didn't say? If yes, discuss it. It's better to do it now while you are both ready to discuss, than later.

Final thoughts to seeking a win-win solution for both of you

If your spouse hasn't read this book, and is not familiar with the win-win solution, what do you do? You ask, you explore until you are absolutely sure. Just use the language patterns as outlined before.

"Let me see if I got you right ..."
"How come this is important to you?"

You might not enjoy the benefit of your partner treating you the same, but at least one of you will do it—you. That is good enough for starters.

For you to be able to reach a win-win solution, you have to have an open mind to your spouse's opinions and desires. You don't have to agree with everything that your spouse says, but you have to be open to considering his or her position.

Pay attention to your own body language. If you find yourself sitting with your arms crossed and shaking your head no-no-no (or just thinking it), when your spouse is trying to explain his or her position, the discussion will not get anywhere.

It surely takes more effort and creativity to reach a satisfying solution, yet in the long run this is essential. When you use a win-win approach, the underlying motivation is to please both of you. The result is an amplified feeling of connection, understanding, support and confidence in your ability to solve any life problem that comes your way. It's such a liberating feeling. It's something you can learn as well.

Exercise

- Think of the last time you had to negotiate what you wanted to do together.
- Which patterns did you use?
- How well did they serve you?
- Were results satisfactory? If not, commit to using a win-win approach to conflict resolution next time.

What If You Screw Up?

By now you have in your love toolbox the essential tools that you can use to prevent things from going wrong. You know how to listen, how to talk mindfully, how to express disagreement constructively and receive complaints gracefully, how to prevent a meltdown and things starting to get out of control and lastly, how to seek a win-win solution.

The reality is that even with all of your best intentions, you will screw things up. That's normal because we are human beings and not robots. We make mistakes and we screw up. In any relationship that's alive and kicking, this is happening.

It doesn't even have to be a product of a disagreement though. It may be a harmless comment that you made, not thinking much about it, yet it left a mark on your partner's face instantly, and you knew you blew it. Therefore, this chapter is not about preventing you from messing things up in the first place, but what you do about it afterwards.

It's about mindful apologizing

Have you ever tried to apologize, but ended up in a much greater fight? You really wanted to apologize, but have said something that really set your partner off?

Knowing when, and especially how, to apologize makes you a better person. It earns you appreciation and respect, while doing the opposite consistently for a long time, earns you a badge of being a jerk. It builds resentment and it becomes very hard for your partner not to start behaving the same.

Most of us were not taught how to apologize properly when we were younger. Remember when we were young and at school, when a teacher would force two kids to apologize, only for the two to stare at the floor and mumble, "Sorry," and not really mean it? As we will learn this is only one step in an apology, but it's not enough.

So how to apologize to your partner? It's a process and not a word. So it's not "I'm sorry, honey," and then walking away, but leaving a feeling that you genuinely care. Only then apologizing becomes a beautiful exercise that, after it's done, connects you and not divides you.

So, how do you do it? Follow these steps:

1. Cool down completely

Only if you are calm, preferably with some time away from the event, proceed.

2. Think about what happened

Here are a couple of ideas to think about:

- How was I feeling at the time?
- Was I in stress? What for?
- What went on in my mind?
- Which concerns did I have?
- What piece of information did I not have at the time?
- What piece of information did I have, but my spouse didn't, and couldn't have at the time?
- What did I do that triggered my spouse?
- What did I learn from this?
- How could I have reacted differently?

- What will I do the next time a similar event occurs?
- How do I wish my spouse would help me? (this is only a wish, but you don't have control over this)

The more objectively you can think of what really happened, the more chances you have to apologize in a calm way, and you will have a much better chance to actually strengthen your relationship.

3. Approach softly

Tell your partner you would like to apologize, and ask if now is an appropriate time.

- "I would like to apologize for _____, if this is a good time?"

A sincere look in your spouse's eyes and a gentle touch does wonders. Show that you care. Show respect and genuine concern.

4. Express regret

- "I am sorry that I _____."

Remember to use *I* and not *you* sentences. Say what you are sorry for, and what you did, and avoid talking about your spouse. In that sense, apologizing is similar to complaining, which we covered. Resort back to that chapter, if in doubt.

- Yes: "I am sorry that *I* have_____."
- No: "I am sorry *you* have gotten mad at me."

Focus on what your part was in all this, and leave the rest to your partner. It happens all too quickly that we start thinking about how poor we are, and if they would do this or that, then everything would be fine. Then we send such messages over to our partner and expect a welcome party.

5. Claim responsibility

Take a deep breath and acknowledge what you did.

- "As much as I hate to admit it, I am responsible for _____ / I am angry at myself for (reacting like that, saying things ...)."

6. Confirm it was non-intentional

- "I really didn't mean to (hurt you ...)."

It's important to say it out loud even though you know, and your spouse may know, that you didn't really mean to hurt him. You were upset and things get said. Nevertheless, words are powerful and they have to be said aloud.

7. Explain the circumstances

Explain what happened and why you think it happened. Just remember all the things that you've collected during your preparation to apologize.

Describe how, in your eyes, things happened and what you think was the trigger. Use your newly acquired skills of talking mindfully. Use *I* sentences and talk about your feelings.

Describe concerns that you've had, and that you think your spouse wasn't aware of at the time.

Loudly give your spouse the benefit of the doubt. Acknowledge that they couldn't have known some things that went on in your mind at the time.

8. Lesson learned

Say what you will do the next time the same or similar event occurs. That counts much more than just a "sorry" because it shows the other person that you have put some thought into it.

If you have a wish for how you would like your partner to react in the future, say it. But be careful. Don't resort to blaming because it might signal to your partner that, in fact, your apology was meaningless! Also, be aware it's just your wish. You don't have control over your partner, you only have full control over yourself!

Final thoughts about apologizing

Take turns. It's not only about knowing how to give an apology properly, but how to receive it. After both of you being upset, it's important that you come together to sort things out. You should be able to say to each other what went wrong and make an apology. Instead of blaming each other, both of your energies go to understanding what happened, soothing each other, and preventing future clashes like this. That's why it's the best practice to take turns and listen to each other.

With some practice, you'll be able to accelerate the process. When you get good at apologizing, you may want to combine certain steps, or do it a quicker way. This is fine as long it serves the purpose. The point is for you to know the core elements and incorporate them into your own unique apology.

As already advised, journaling helps a lot, especially at preventing similar mistakes in the future. I have a habit of asking myself in my journal each week, the same set of questions. What did I learn of my self? What did I learn of others? What will I do the same or differently next time? Those are exactly the questions that lead you to a much-needed reflection of what you can do differently to change things for the better. Journaling will speed things up and make you a better person.

Don't forget to watch your language, and talk mindfully. Use touch, a hug. Look your partner in the eyes. If accepting an apology, be a good listener.

If your spouse is not familiar with this concept (yet), worry not. Just apologize in a new way and they will learn it from you. I guarantee you that you will not get rejected for apologizing mindfully, so you really don't have anything to lose, but a lot to gain.

Finally, even though this section is about knowing how to apologize, I want to share something important. Don't wait for an "I'm sorry" to begin the process of forgiving. The natural outcome of creating a loving and friendly atmosphere is that forgiveness becomes continual. It becomes built into the fabric of the relationship. When an upsetting event happens within the relationship, it's seen as a slight, not an assault. And when one is aware of the good in the other, it's easier to let go of the times when the other shows their humanity in their mistakes. Forgiveness is not about forgetting though. It's about remembering an upsetting event through non-judgmental eyes, giving your spouse the benefit of the doubt.

Summary

1. Cool down

2. Think what happened

3. Approach softly

4. Express regret

5. Claim responsibility

6. Confirm it was non-intentional

7. Explain the circumstances

8. Lesson learned

Exercise

Get something to write on and follow the next steps:

Think back to a time when you had an incident. Regardless of whose fault it may have been, for the next exercise, craft out an apology on your part.

Step 1. Think about what happened.

Now it's time to work on your side of the apology.

Step 2. Approach softly. Write down your opener. "I would like to apologize for _____, if this is the right time?"

Step 3. Express your regret. What will you say to explain what it is that you regret having done? "I'm sorry that _____."

Step 4. Claim responsibility. "As much as it's hard to admit, I am responsible / I am angry at myself for _____."

Step 5. Confirm you didn't mean any harm. "I really didn't mean to _____."

Step 6. Explain the circumstances. Use the things you discovered in Step 1.

Step 7. Explain to your partner what you learned and how you will react next time.

Read it out loud. How does it feel? If you were the one to hear the apology, how would you react?

Get Over It and Get On
With Feeling Good

In previous chapters, I discussed how to solve everyday conflicts effectively. This is great as the vast majority of problems, issues and disagreements we have in our lives actually are of an everyday nature. Solving everyday conflicts successfully does contribute to a friendly atmosphere.

If every day problems could be considered small (but not unimportant), and therefore kittens, the problems that I will talk about here are the gorillas. They are harder to conquer.

You must have noticed that sometimes, while having a pretty minor disagreement, something strange happens. At first you seemed to be disagreeing about a relatively small issue, yet somehow things got nasty. You ended in a big, nasty fight. Some fights just seem to come from nowhere.

I like to compare this to a giant tornado that suddenly evolves from a normal summer storm. Next thing you know, the wind picks up, and debris (accusations) picked up from everywhere (memory, past events), is all mixed up in an unrecognizable mass, flying around with great speeds, hitting you from all sides.

Then there are cases when the tornado happens somewhere else: inside you. On the outside, nothing much is visible, but inside you, things are boiling and spinning fast.

If something like this is happening on a recurring basis, then this is a good indication that you may be looking at a bigger problem. You can't overcome it by applying the same methods for an ordinary, everyday conflict, because here we're getting much more personal. We are being hit directly at our core and our self-worth is threatened.

This is when the problems start, and the first step is to recognize it.

Signs that you are looking at a bigger problem:

- You experience a surprisingly strong emotional and physical reaction.
- Your heart starts pumping, your face gets red, your hands start to sweat and your whole body gets tense as if you were preparing for a real fight (which in reality is exactly what your body is doing).
- You get literally flushed over by feelings of distrust, rejection, shame, disrespect and resentment.
- Your partner looks surprised, and tells you that you are overreacting.
- You may be surprised at yourself as well.

Further signs:

- After the conversation, you feel even more hurt and rejected by your partner.

- Talking just makes things worse. It seems the more you talk about it, the less progress you make.

- The more time goes on, the more negative feelings you have about your partner.

- It seems like both of you have gotten entrenched in your positions and you're leading a war of some kind. No one is ready to compromise, not a tiny bit. Eventually you give up and stop talking all together.

Most likely such a problem has been around troubling your relationship for quite some time. Surely, it did not just appear from nowhere. As you will most likely discover later in this chapter, many such problems do indeed have roots in the past. You are experiencing some issues and disagreements, which in fact symbolize deeper conflicts between the two of you.

So, is it about solving problems stemming from the past? I think not. I also believe it's not necessary either.

Take for example my friend who had his left knee damaged from a skiing accident years ago. He can still live a very rich and rewarding life, as long as he doesn't make skiing a central part of it. That's all there is to it.

It's not about solving problems, but overcoming them by understanding the driving forces behind them, and then reacting in a different way so they stop bothering you.

Do my wife and I have disagreements? Sure we do. I would be seriously concerned if we didn't. And yes, even though we know each other's triggers pretty well by now, we still step on each other's toes occasionally, albeit not intentionally. And yes, we do get uneasy, if not, angry.

What makes all the difference is that we are now both aware of what is going on in our heads. Some also say it's a conscious relationship, because it's a deliberate act of being aware of what's going on. That is what I want you to learn here. I want you to acquire the knowledge and skills necessary to talk about almost anything, even the most toxic stuff, and to find your way out of it while maintaining your connection at the same or even a higher level.

To my experience, this changes everything. The ability to do that builds up the confidence in yourself and in your relationship. Mastering what you are about to read next will give you the confidence to face and solve practically any difficult or otherwise toxic issue you have now or might have in the future.

There is another funny thing that happens when you become aware of the things in your and your partner's heads. Negative feelings and thoughts that you used to have about your partner when they stepped on your toes, the anger that you used to experience to the point that you started wondering if you married to right person, starts fading away very quickly.

All those negative feelings melt away in front of your very eyes. When you think of some of the exhausting fights you've had in the past, it becomes silly and makes you want to smile.

The moment you both truly understand the underlying issues behind your conflicts, all the arguing, negative thoughts, nasty fighting and many other unpleasant things that went on and on for many years if not decades, start making sense. As a consequence those exact fights lose their power and can become obsolete.

This is exactly what happened in my relationship.

The knowledge and skills that you are about to learn in the continuation of this chapter are simple in their nature. I didn't say easy because that would mean they require no effort. The things that you are about to read do require some conscious effort. Yet the effort you will invest will be paid back so many times that you will ask yourself why you didn't do this before.

After both of you get familiar with a technique that I am about to explain in this section, and try it out a couple of times successfully, you will become a therapist to each other instead of having to rely on a marriage therapist or counselor, while spending lots of money to get a questionable outcome.

So what will we do next?

I will help you discover some things about your childhood. Then, you will become aware of frustrations that you have about your partner. Lastly, you will learn how to overcome those frustrations or at least minimize them to an acceptable level.

A Short Introduction to Yourself

As explained, successful and happy couples know the underlying issues behind some of their behaviors.

They know each other's wounds, as well as dreams from their childhoods, and they have empathy for them. They do not feel sorry for their partner, rather they show empathy for their partner's wounds! Successful couples can truly put themselves in each other's shoes and understand the reasons that trigger their partners to act as they do.

Those triggers could just be because you're tired. But if tensions are of a recurring nature, then they are very likely triggered by current experiences that bear a resemblance to ways in which you'd been hurt or treated in the past. An example is when your partner takes a tone with you that is similar to the tone of an important adult from your childhood who was responsible for creating a particular pain in you. Sometimes, we have to think long and hard in order to make these connections, but the exercise below will make it a little easier.

It's important that you do this exercise. At first alone, and then, when the time is right, with both of you. It's human nature that makes it almost impossible for us to get influenced by another person unless we feel that that person understands us. So before you think of changing the way your partner behaves, ask yourself if you truly understand him. And the same goes another way. If either (or both) of you feel judged, misunderstood or rejected by the other, you will not be able to manage the problems in your marriage on a sustainable basis. You will get caught in cyclical fights as I was with my wife before we understood this.

Just think for a moment. Wouldn't it be great? Wouldn't it be great to stop having those nasty tornado-like fights? Wouldn't it be great to be able to release all the pressure inside you that's accumulated over the years?

This is what we are going to do in the next section.

As I have already stressed, I'm going to give you clues to what is happening now, and then moving on with your life.

Why childhood?

It's widely believed that childhood is the most impactful time for human beings because it's when most of our core beliefs, values and behaviors are formed. By saying childhood, we assume the ages of newborn up to nineteen, with men slightly above twenty years of age. But it doesn't need to be only childhood. It can also be a powerful experience with your first boss at your first job, or the death of a family member, a frightening experience sometime in the past, or some other impactful experience that left an important mark on your life.

Having said that, make no mistake. I am not going to tell you that you have been somehow abused in your childhood, and you might not know about it. This reminds me of a joke that goes like this:

Therapist: "You were abused as a child, but you don't know it."

Client: "Hmm, I don't?"

Therapist: "See, I told you!"

I am not going to do that. I am not going dredge up your past only to make you feel a bit better by feeling sorry for yourself. Your parents have probably made a couple of mistakes, the same as you have or will in the future. You parents gave you all the love they had, and have done everything they had knowledge of. Your parents gave you everything that they could.

It's all about the awareness of knowing what's going on in your subconscious and, later on, in the subconscious of your spouse. When you become aware of this, it becomes much easier to start seeing things from a different perspective and behaving differently.

Also, we will focus on you and only you. But, in order for your spouse to understand you, you first have to understand yourself.

So, as we have that clarified, let's concentrate on discovering some interesting stuff about a time when you were a kid.

Exercise – Understanding yourself

We are going to do a very simple exercise. It doesn't require any special preparations aside from some sheets of blank paper and some peace. Even if you are reading this book with your partner, you have to do this exercise separately.

Before you start, take a moment to relax. Take a deep breath a couple of times, hold your breath for a few seconds, and then breathe out slowly. Repeat three times, and then you are set to go.

Now, take a piece of paper and start writing:

- Memories: list your positive memories from your childhood.
- Feelings: list how you felt as a child at that time.
- Frustrations: list recurring childhood frustrations such as, I was ignored, I was always getting into trouble, I felt invisible, etc. What were you missing at that time?
- Responses: list your responses to these frustrations. How did you cope with them? What did you typically do? (For example: screamed or yelled, went to my room, I went out with friends, I went silent, etc.)

You're surely thinking you couldn't remember everything. And you probably didn't. But you did the most important ones, and you can come back later and add new findings.

Share your childhood memories with your partner

You might be in a relationship for years or just a couple of months. It really doesn't matter because frustrations from childhood are generally not shared among couples as freely as one would imagine.

So it was in my own case. After more than a decade of marriage, my wife and I finally got insight into each other's frustrations and wounds from the past. We were stunned to hear the stories from each other, but just as surprised that we didn't know them already after so many years of life together.

It's a person's ability to be vulnerable, while sharing their deepest fears and frustrations with another person, that is a very good indicator of how strong their relationship is.

I believe it must have something to do with how our society perceives the sharing of our deepest fears with another human being. This especially holds true for men who are supposed to be strong and rock solid as if sharing stuff with their spouse would make them less strong. In my experience, it's actually the opposite.

Exercise

- Make sure you've got an hour or two of uninterrupted time together.
- Make sure you are both relaxed. As a matter of fact, you should feel a bit of anticipation because you will soon find

out something about your spouse that you probably
didn't know.

- Now, tell, your spouse what you found out in the previous
  exercise.

- Take turns.

- When listening, listen actively. You don't have to
  summarize, but listen and ask questions like, "How did you
  feel?"

How do you feel now?

Map Your Frustrations

The next exercise builds on the "Understanding yourself" exercise in
the previous section.

After the exercise that you are about to do next, you will have a
detailed map of what bothers you in your relationship, a higher
awareness of how you feel about it, what your typical responses are
and, most important, an understanding of why you react as you do.
Finishing the exercise below will bring you one big step closer to
understanding what it is that you actually need.

In my case, it was five frustrations that I had with my wife. As you
will discover, some frustrations will overlap, and in reality, you
probably have only two or three frustrations from your past. Those
are the ones that, when touched by your partner or someone else
unintentionally, make you feel bad and cause you to react in your
own way.

Exercise

Refer to the example table below and start filling out your own. I suggest that you simply take an empty sheet of paper and divide it into columns, like the template below. Myself, being a bit on the technological side, found it easier to use an Excel spreadsheet for this, as odd as it sounds.

Each row is reserved for one frustration. Start with the most pressing one.

- Column A: Think of a recurring behavior of your partner that frustrates you the most. If you could let it out, criticize and, if needed, shout at your partner. What would you say?

  Here and only here is it allowed to directly criticize and put into statements phrases like, "You never _____." "You always _____."

- Column B: When your partner behaves like this, how does it make you feel?

- Column C: What's your usual response?

- Column D: What are you actually afraid of? Why does it bother you so much? Refer back to the exercise where you identified childhood frustrations and your responses, and see if there are similarities. Odds are there are.

- Column E: What would you wish instead? What is your deepest wish related to this particular frustration? Use short sentences. Focus on what you want and minimize "don't want" sentences.

A. Behavior that frustrates me You ... never ..., always ...	B. My feelings When you do this, I feel ...	C. My typical reaction Then I react like ...	D. To hide my fear from...	E. My desire I wish ...
It frustrates me when you avoid talking. When I invite you to have a chat, you roll your eyes. All I hear is "Not now, I need five minutes for my self." If eventually you do talk, you show little interest, except when we talk about your job. On an average day, you spend more time talking to your friends than you do with me in a whole week.	I am angry because I come last. I feel I'm being taken for granted and I feel rejected. I feel I didn't deserve this.	Most of the time I say nothing because I don't want to fight again. When you really piss me off, I will sarcastically say, "It seems like watching stupid TV shows is more important to you."	Fear of being taken for granted as I was when I was a kid.	I wish we could spend more time just talking, and I wish you would initiate the talk.

This was an example of a filled-out template for one frustration. In your case, it will probably be a couple of them, but there's nothing wrong if you write ten or more. The more you let it out, the more awareness you will have about yourself, and the more you will start seeing patterns in your behavior and responses.

If you have done the exercise above, you now have a pretty good picture, practically a map of your frustrations with your partner.

You have just done an invaluable service to yourself. You got to know yourself better, and that is important before expecting your partner to understand you better.

By now, hopefully your partner has established a similar list as well. If not I will have to ask you not to continue with this chapter. This is fine as well. Just continue practicing what you have learned by now. Persist. The time will come when your partner will be ready to read this book, and this particular section, and do the above exercise themselves.

In any case, do not share this with your spouse just yet, not until you learn an extremely efficient tool that allows you to share your frustrations with each other in a safe way. It's called the intentional dialogue.

The Intentional Dialogue

Intentional dialogue, also called Imago Dialogue, was developed by Dr. Harville Hendrix and his wife, Dr. Helen LaKelly Hunt, the creators of Imago Relationship Theory. The process was formulated through extensive studies of psychological theories of relationships and clinical work with couples.

My wife and I used intentional dialogue during the initial phases of our reconciliation, to discuss our frustrations with each other. Otherwise, I am afraid, we wouldn't have been able to end a conversation without accusations and arguing. We were just not that far yet. In that sense the intentional dialogue is beautiful, because its structure prevents you from screwing things up.

The essence of intentional dialogue is a conversation in which people agree to listen to others without judgment, and accept their views as equally valid as their own.

The most powerful benefit that this provides is a safe structure to talk about things that you couldn't talk through for many years, if ever. Instead of worrying when your partner will hit you back, or expecting a fight to start any minute, you focus on telling your partner what it is that really bothers you, and your partner listens, maybe for the very first time. That is, I tell you, a big relief and a fantastic achievement.

My experience showed me that, after using intentional dialogue to talk about our most pressing frustrations, things changed. My wife and I got much more connected, and we both felt a big relief. Finally, we were able to say what we had wanted to say for so long, but couldn't. Now we can.

Should I start with intentional dialogue?

On a practical level, it takes a certain amount of connection before you start with intentional dialogue. This is why it's important you follow the book in the order that it was written. If you've been doing the exercises in this book, and in the order of the chapters, you should now be in better shape as a couple. On the other hand, if you have not seen any progress in your relationship yet, insisting on starting an intentional dialogue would be the same as putting a coach in front of the horses. I don't recommend it. That is also why intentional dialogue is covered exactly here and not at the beginning of the book.

Therefore, if you feel that either of you is not prepared yet, don't force it. You probably need more time. Just continue to practice the principles as covered in previous chapters. With persistence and some additional time, your efforts will start showing effects, and that will be a good moment to jointly revisit this chapter as well.

What's the goal?

I feel it's necessary for you to understand that it's not the immediate resolution to your frustrations that we are after here. Even though that would be fantastic, it's not what really happens. Your main goal is to connect, and start thinking differently about one another by changing your perception of the other.

You are basically looking for an "aha" moment in your mind. It's when a behavior of your spouse that used to drive you crazy starts to make sense. It's the point when you start to finally get it.

You will start to understand the reasons for the behavior of your partner that has made you so miserable and angry in the past. In retrospect, many of the fights you had have a deeper reason. As a result, you both are starting to develop empathy for each other's needs.

You'll also understand that it's not your partner who wanted to hurt you, but it's their wounds from the past that made them behave in a certain way, while not being aware of it. Your partner is a human being just like you. Sometimes this is hard to understand.

Your new understanding of things will make room for new perceptions that will replace those that you once had about each other. In my experience, this is a crucial point in any relationship that is in trouble, as was in my case.

As I've mentioned, it's mostly an overly negative perception that partners have of one another that is killing their relationship. If you have a negative picture of your partner in your head, and you are constantly looking for yet more proof that your partner is _____ (fill in the blank with your common criticism), then you will keep finding proof that it's really so. Things will never be any different than they are today.

As your perception of your partner changes, your feelings about one another change as well. You start replacing the negative feelings with empathy and understanding. When this happens, you've stopped the self-feeding, negative, vicious cycle pushing your relationship downwards, and you'll start to slowly spin it in the opposite, the positive, direction. You have started a positive, reinforced loop, instead of the previous negative one, because you know what the underlying issues of your frustrations are with each other. When this happens, you are much more willing to reach out and help each other. Just think for a moment, wouldn't that be great?

Finally, we have come to the intentional dialogue itself. It has a very strict structure that you should follow so you can't make mistakes.

That said, don't worry. I will not tell you to learn some complicated script. Firstly, you can always print out the script. And secondly, as you will find out later, when you master the core idea, in my experience, you will not need a strict structure anymore.

The core elements

You actually already know the core elements of the intentional dialogue because we have already covered them. You know the concept of using *I* and *I feel* sentences. You probably also remember the section about listening skills that we covered. See, nothing is new!

It's the *structure* that is so interesting, because, as I have mentioned, it makes the receiver of the message actively listen, and the sender of the message talk in a certain, nonthreatening way.

At the same time, intentional dialogue is aimed at discovering underlying issues that led to the problem in the first place, and developing the empathy of the listener, and the structure ties it all together in a logical path. It makes sense to have a difficult conversation this way. This is also my own experience.

So let's go quickly through the core elements of intentional dialogue.

1. Mirroring and summarizing

Mirroring is a way of listening by which the receiver (the person receiving the message) echoes the sender's message as accurately as possible.

Imagine that you are talking to a friend, and you really want to memorize everything that is being said, so you repeat loudly what your friend just said. That's what we are looking for.

- Sender: "I feel frustrated when you don't call me during the entire day."
- Receiver (mirroring): "You feel frustrated when I don't call you during the entire day."

Mirroring helps the receiver listen to what the sender is actually saying, rather than thinking already of his or her response.

Along the way, you encourage your partner by saying:

- "Tell me more!"
- "Is there anything else?"

When your partner answers with "No, I think that is all," then you do a summary by saying:

- "So, correct me if I am wrong, but what you're actually saying is ..."
- "Let me see if I got you right. What you're saying is that ..."

2. Validating

Validating means saying:

- "That makes sense to me, because ..."
- "From your perspective, it makes sense."

Please note, you *don't* have to agree with you partner. It's not your job to agree to anything.

Your job is to suspend your judgment for a little while, and show respect for your partner's view. Remember, it's your partner's map of the world and your partner's perception of things. They have the same right to think it's the right view as you do.

It doesn't matter who is right or wrong over a particular issue, because we're looking beyond that. We're looking for underlying pain! After validating, take a look at your partner's face and body. Very often there is a visible sign of relief.

3. Empathy

Empathy is about putting yourself in your partner's shoes.

It's about you saying, "I can imagine how that _____ (insert core frustration or your partner's childhood story) made you feel _____ (insert feeling)." or "You must have been feeling _____ (insert feeling)."

The three wishes

Okay, so you have your list of frustrations, and there are things you wish your partner would change, or do, more (or less). In the script below, you'll find a way to state this desire without triggering a rejection.

Your job is to think of three wishes that your partner will be able to pick from. By your partner fulfilling one of those, it will give you the feeling that you've missed so much.

Example: You feel taken for granted. One of your wishes that will help you overcome this feeling could be like this:

"For the duration of the next four weeks, if you are going to be late coming home for more than thirty minutes, you will call me at least half an hour before and notify me about the change."

Then think of and write down two other wishes, and formulate them in the same fashion.

Your partner's job is to pick any of those wishes at his or her sole discretion, and commit to doing it for the duration requested.

Attention!

Fulfilling one of the three wishes by either partner doesn't mean that either of you is right or wrong.

It's simply a gift from one partner to another. A temporary token of good will, if you want. But it will get your relationship spinning in the right direction.

How to formulate your three wishes.

While thinking of the wishes, follow these rules on how to formulate them. A wish has to satisfy the following criteria:

- Specific (I want you to give me a hug)
- Measurable (Well, it's a hug, you either give it or not)
- Attainable (Think baby steps. For example, a hug is not a complicated thing to do. You don't need your partner to learn to fly a space shuttle!)
- Relevant (It has to address the particular *underlying* fear, need or desire)
- Time bound (Every day, after I come from work for the next three weeks)

Further notes:

- Think baby steps.

- Let them be small enough so your partner says, "I can do that!" and not, "Oh my God, how the hell am I going to do any of these?"

- The three wishes should be limited in duration to a maximum of three or four weeks.

Even after your partner decides to fulfill one of your wishes, this doesn't mean that the underlying issue of the frustration will somehow miraculously go away. But this is okay. Remember, by being willing to fulfill each other's wishes, you are starting to change the direction your relationship is spinning, and start the healing process.

Even though the wishes are time bound, from my experience a funny thing happens. Once you begin doing something for your spouse for a couple of weeks, many times you may discover that it's actually not so hard, especially after you see how much positive energy it sparks. Seeing how happy your spouse is, and how much better your relationship is because of those little things that you voluntarily do for your spouse, you keep doing it even after the bound period of time lapses.

In certain cases you will experience, not only that you are doing the thing that you picked from your partner's wish list, but also that you are fulfilling the other two wishes as well, even though you don't have to.

Exercise:

Pick the most pressing issue from your list of frustrations and do the following:

Frustration:

_____

My Three Wishes are:

1. _____

2. _____

3. _____

The script of the intentional dialogue

I am about to show you the template that I have used when I was at the beginning of my reconciliation with my wife. I have found it to be perfect for telling each other the frustrations we had, as well as for telling our wishes for a change in behavior in a safe way within the same conversation.

In that sense, the script below is a combination of intentional dialogue as developed by Dr. Hendrix and Dr. Hunt, and a so-called behavior change request.

Have a look at the example below and familiarize yourself with it. It's so detailed because I want to give you a full script that works, so you don't get lost the first time. You can print it out and have it in your hand when you do it the first couple of times, same as my wife and I did.

Sender	Receiver
1. Ask to have an intentional dialogue. "I would like to have a talk with you about ... (keep it short). Is now a good time?"	
	2. Accommodate the request at least within 24 hours.
3. Say your frustration <u>in one sentence</u>. Keep it short and be direct. "I am frustrated when you avoid talking to me." "It really bothers me when you ..."	4. Take a deep breath. Prepare to listen non-judgementally, without thinking what your response will be. "Go on, I'm ready to listen."
	5. Mirror and check for correctness. "You said ..." "I heard you saying ..." "Have I heard you right?"
6. Describe your frustration. "I feel frustrated when you ..." "When you do ... I feel ..." "What hurts me the most is ... " "When this happens, I think of you ..." "And when this happens my feelings about you are ..." "I usually react ... ... and I do so because ..."	7. Just summarize by saying: "If I got you right, you are frustrated when I ... , is that it?" Your partner might say: "Well you missed this ... and that ..." In that case, listen and summarize the whole story again.
	8. Ask about the childhood. "How do these feelings remind you of your past experiences in your childhood?"

9. Look at your list of frustrations. "When I feel like that, it reminds me of … (from your childhood)." "The thing that hurt me the most when I was a child was … " "I felt …" "I was afraid that …" "To protect myself I used to … (your typical response)." "What I needed the most at the time but didn't get, was …"	10. Summarize "When you feel like … it reminds you …" And then try to summarize your partner's pain from his or her childhood. "Have I got it right?" If not, let your partner correct you, and summarize again
	11. Ask "What do you truly desire in our relationship?"
12. Tell your desire that is relevant to your frustration. "I just wish …"	13. Mirror and at the end make a quick summary. Validate by saying "I understand." "I hear what you're saying." "Yes, sometimes (often) I do what you're saying …" "It makes sense … because in your childhood …" "Knowing this makes sense, that you want … from me." Show empathy: "You must be feeling … " "You deserve … (insert your partner's deepest desire)." "What specifically can I do for you?"
14. State your three wishes. One of those will be your partner's gift to you. Example of a wish: Every day for the next three weeks, I want you to give me a smile the first time you see me. State all three wishes.	15. Mirror each of the wishes and check for correctness.

	16. Pick one wish that you intend to fulfill, and tell your partner, "My gift to you is ... (the one you picked)."
17. Thank your partner. Say "Thank you for being prepared to do this for me. It will help me overcome ... (part of the story with a relevant pain from your childhood)."	
18. " ... and this will help me cope with my fear of ... (that you currently have)."	
19. " ... and I hope in the future I will be able to feel ... (insert what you want to feel in the future in your relationship)." Remember to say what feeling you do want to have in the future and not the feeling you don't want.	
	20. Say "You're always welcome and I am happy to do this for you."

Note:

It might be a good idea to download the intentional dialogue script directly from your members area. You can find it here:

http://geni.us/fgmbonus

Now it's your turn!

Pick one of your frustrations from your list and do this on your own.

When you finish, pay attention for a moment and observe your feeling of closeness and connection.

Then both share this with each other:

- "At this very moment, what I feel about you is …"
- "One thing that I've noticed during this dialogue is …"

Then, you can switch roles only when your partner explains their point of view of the same frustration.

Repeat the process.

Hints for the sender

- Prepare before starting to have a dialogue.
- Write down the exact points as written in point six of the script just seen.
- Prepare your three wishes.
- Then follow the script.
- Talk about how you feel and do not blame your spouse or partner. Talk like you would talk to your friend.
- Mind your language. Use your newly acquired knowledge of talking mindfully, and you'll be just fine.

Hints for the receiver

Listening is actually the hardest part of the job. You might not agree to everything that will be said, but you still have to follow the intentional dialogue structure.

Your job is to listen carefully, mirror, summarize, validate and show empathy, while encouraging your partner to open up and tell you what's on their mind, *without fear of being judged.* Failing to do so, you are taking the risk of finding yourself in the same old pattern that didn't work.

- Try matching the words and phrases your partner has used as closely as possible. Especially at mirroring, avoid adding your own twists to the story.

- That's why I strongly advise to take notes as your partner talks. Write down your partner's key phrases. As you echo back your partner's ways of saying things, your partner will feel heard and appreciated.

- Most likely, you will occasionally have a hard time catching up. Don't worry. You can always stop your spouse, mirror and summarize, and have them move on when you are ready. The partner that is doing the talking, when seeing the other one is actively listening, is more than prepared to wait.

- Do not judge, not even in your mind. It's especially tempting to the untrained listener to start thinking of a response or get angry. Some things you will not agree with. Some may sound even outrageous to you. You don't have to agree with what was said. Remember, this is how your partner sees and feels about things. It's not about you now. Also, bear in mind that this is about discovering the underlying issues. They show themselves in different outfits and disguises, just open your mind and pay attention.

- Think of your spouse in a way that they love you and they don't want to hurt you.

- Remember the good listening skills you have just learned.

- Don't forget to encourage your partner by saying, "Tell me more." or "Is there anything else?"

Schedule some uninterrupted time in advance

Especially at the beginning of the healing process, you have your of frustrations and you want to clear them up. That's the whole point, right?

My experience shows that it's best to pick a day in a month to discuss your frustrations in advance, and then stick to it. Say every first Sunday evening in the month, at 9:00 p.m. Block this time and do not let everyday stuff run over your time for intentional dialogue.

How many months you will need depends on how long your list of frustrations is. As mentioned before, frustrations on your list tend to overlap. Take a close look at your list of frustrations. You can probably merge some of the frustrations and cut down the number to about five to six of the most important frustrations, maybe even less. Start with the most pressing one.

Once per month, two hours is enough, although it happened that my wife and I talked long into the night. Make sure you take turns. If not right now, then the next month. Take it easy and do not expect miracles. Don't do this if one of you is in stress. For that reason, Sunday evenings worked well for me.

When to Use the Intentional Dialogue

My own experience shows that after using intentional dialogue to overcome your most pressing frustrations, you get much more connected than you can ever imagine.

That said, it is my experience that intentional dialogue is <u>not</u> practical for every day issues and smaller disagreements.

You will be the judge if that holds true for you. For handling any other disagreements and issues, my wife and I use the principles covered in earlier chapters. We use the intentional dialogue exclusively to handle bigger problems and frustrations; when one of us notices recurring bad feelings about the other, and wants to discuss it in a controlled and calm manner.

On the other hand, I can only recommend using core elements of intentional dialogue, especially summarizing, validation and empathy even in your daily interactions with your partner, as well as with any other people.

It makes you a more pleasurable person to be with. Summarizing someone's thoughts shows respect. It shows you are really listening. Validating and acknowledging that, from your partner's perspective, things make sense, is a highly connecting exercise. It's a sign of high emotional intelligence. And lastly, what is wrong with showing empathy and telling people that you can, in fact, imagine how they must have felt?

Peek Into Your
Feel Good Future Together

An intimate personal relationship with another person is the most important decision you make in your life, as it affects and determines your health, personal growth and professional development much more than you think. Yet, too many people just let it happen, and watch on the side as if this life was not theirs, but someone else's.

In that sense, too many couples are just passive spectators, watching their lives together unfold one day at a time. They may plan their respective education and their careers, the building of a new home, or even a vacation, but it never occurs to them to think and decide together what they want from their life and their relationship. As a result, many end up discouraged and disillusioned, wondering where they went wrong.

I was like that. Even though my wife and I have walked through bits and pieces of something that we call a vision of our marriage, we have never taken the time to really think about it deliberately and write it down. We have never clearly answered these questions:

- What do we want as a couple?
- Why do we want it?
- What do we need to do in order to get there?
- What is most important?
- How will we know if we are moving in the right direction?

These are very simple questions, yet answering them may not be so easy.

As we all know, change is the only constant in life. Are you going to choose the direction your life will take, and the kind of person you will become, or will you just sit back and wait for life to happen to you?

If you want to create something different for your life and your relationship, it's not enough to just know what you don't want. You also need to know what you DO want, and you need to be able to articulate it in a clear and compelling vision that you both believe in.

The thing is, if you haven't consciously and clearly articulated what you want, your picture of your future together is blurry at best. Our brains seek for what's familiar, and so they resist what's unfamiliar and vague. If you're not clear about what you want to create, then you'll lack the motivation to act because you'd rather stay with your current familiar reality. You will end up doing more of the same, which is what led you to this situation in the first place.

This is where your vision of your relationship kicks in. It unifies your dreams in a story that propels you forward, and motivates you to do the changes necessary for your relationship to grow.

That said, it's certainly possible to have a stable marriage without a shared vision of your relationship. As a matter of fact, many couples do, even very happy couples. If you foster a friendly atmosphere such us spending time together, talking together and doing those little, nice things for each other often enough, if you know how to listen to each other as well as say what you have to say mindfully, if you have learned how to handle disagreements well, then you are ahead of the vast majority of couples. You have your relationship in pretty good shape, probably in much better shape than most of your friends.

Then again, ask yourself: What is the purpose of all this? Being able to overcome disagreements in a connecting way is certainly great, but what higher purpose does it serve? Are we in our relationship to get along nicely and get through life with the smallest number of bruises? Or is there some higher meaning?

On the part of my wife and myself, we did eventually write down our marriage vision, but only after more than a decade of marriage. I wish we had done it before. Then again-it's never too late. If you haven't done it by now, I strongly encourage you to do that.

As I explained at the beginning of the book, human brains need direction. You will figure out what you have to do once you know where you want to go. You will figure out how to do it with a little help from this book, but the direction can come only from yourself, or in this case from both of you.

The next set of exercises is dedicated to developing a vision of your relationship, *your feel good future together.* It will build on what you have already determined earlier in the book, when you were asked to think of what you want from your marriage. This will now come in handy, because you will build on that, and put the pieces from both of you together into a vision of your marriage.

Exercise

Step 1. (alone)

Make a list with short statements about your ideal relationship. Begin sentences with *we*, and make them short and positive. Use present tense. Include everything that is already positive and ongoing in your relationship, as well as things that you wish for. Assign each statement a degree of importance from one to five, whereas five is most important and one the least important.

Look for sample statements below to spark some ideas, but generally you may want to start with aspects of your relationship (how do you relate to each other, spending time together, conversations, keeping the relationship interesting and fun) and then work out through areas of your life together that might be important, such as children (how will you raise your kids), relations to your extended family and in-laws, work and careers (for example, how will you support each other), finances, where and how do you want to live and (if you practice any form of it) spirituality, to name just a few.

Sample vision statements

- We spend time together
- We have regular fun together
- We take time daily to talk about our thoughts, feelings and stories
- We handle our disagreements calmly
- We have wonderful sex
- We trust each other
- We do nice, little things for each other every day
- We believe in each other
- We support each other in personal and professional growth
- We take care of our bodies
- We are financially independent

- Our kids are happy and content
- We feel safe with each other
- We cultivate ties with extended family and loved ones

Step 2. (alone)

Exchange lists and compare. Mark statements you both agree with. Look for meaning, not exact wording. Mark also statements you don't agree with, but leave that for now.

Step 3. (together)

Prepare a separate list that will now contain only statements of your marriage vision that you both agree with, sorted by degree of importance for both. Include statements that your partner came up with, and that you agree with.

Step 4. (together)

Take a look at your newly born vision of your marriage. Reorder the statements as you both see fit. In case of doubt, look at assigned degrees of importance for both of you for a particular statement and compare totals with other statements. That should give you a rough idea of where to put a particular statement. Don't complicate. This is not an exercise in mathematics. It's much more important to agree on what you will focus on in the future than the exact order of importance.

Try to clarify the statements you don't agree on. Maybe there is only a misunderstanding of the wording used and a rephrase is required. If you get stuck, leave it out completely. It's better to focus on what is common than think too much about what's different. As you focus on positive stuff, things will change anyway.

Step 5. (together)

Pick one of the more important vision statements, yet also the one that seems to be the easiest to attain. Answer the questions in the worksheet below. Put the worksheet somewhere handy so you can see it every day, for example stick it to the inner side of your wardrobe. Even though it might seem a bit odd, write in present tense!

ACTION SHEET

VISION STATEMENT:

_____

(Pick one from the list developed in Step 1.)

1. What specific behavior are we practicing to make our vision come true? What specifically are we doing every day / every week / every month to make it happen?

_____

_____

2. How do we know we are there? What do we see, hear or feel once we have fulfilled our vision?

_____

_____

3. What is the result when we are there?

_____

_____

Start doing it.

Revisit it in three weeks and check how you are doing. If you need to add or change stuff that you are doing, do it.

Note:

You can also download a ready-made worksheet from your members area by visiting http://geni.us/fgmbonus.

Example

Vision statement: "We have regular fun together"

What specific behavior are we practicing to make our vision come true? What specifically are we doing every day / every week / every month to make it happen?

- Once per week we cook together.
- Fridays we have a date. We take turns with who is responsible for organizing it.
- Every Saturday we play a funny game.

What do we see, hear, smell and feel?

- We smile. We laugh every day.
- We feel excitement, pleasure and happiness.

What happens as a result of this?

- We feel connected. We enjoy each other's company. We are looking forward to seeing each other.

Make It Stick

Habits are created by repetition of certain behaviors. It's the habits that close the loop, because habits make good things and changes you've done in your relationship stick. When you have a habit of doing something right for your relationship, it becomes who you really are. They make it possible for your relationship to truly become healthy AND a lasting one.

Your relationship is special

You've probably noticed that in certain places in the book I've used the word *ritual*. It's because with the word ritual I had more of a ceremony in mind, something that's a bit more special. It's a deliberate act through which we show respect to what we're doing.

You may still call them habits if you like, but to my understanding of the word ritual, there is more to it. There is some secrecy. To other couples who haven't yet figured it out, it looks almost like magic; how can you still be so connected after so many years?

The essential rituals

Let's recap the essential habits from this book that will make your relationship really special and have the potential to become your rituals.

1. Do some nice, little thing for your spouse every day. Remember, nice, little things can also be just a genuine smile or   a   simple "Thank you for..."

2. Surprise your spouse regularly. Once per month is okay, but if you manage to do it more often, even better.

Hint: Establish a notebook "The Little Things for Him/ Her" where you write down all the little things that make your spouse happy, as well as ideas for future surprises. Use guidelines as discussed earlier in the book and have a peek regularly for ideas when you need them.

3. At the end of each workday have a "Honey, how was your day?" conversation.

4. Bi-weekly or at least once a month talk about your relationship and your relationship only. It's better to keep the conversation short (around one hour per event is more than okay), but do it regularly.

5. Spend dedicated time together. Have some fun. Once a week is great, but a bi-weekly schedule will serve the purpose as well. Once or twice per year, go somewhere nice,

just the two of you, without kids. It doesn't have to be expensive! The goal is to just hang out together and spend a couple of days together as a couple. Plan it far in advance and block it off in your calendar.

So there you have it. It's five habits that we can also call rituals. Establish these rituals, keep them alive and you'll be golden. And the good part is that you can start right now, and you don't have to do them all at once.

Next, I will mention a couple of other habits and rituals that I've developed over time. I highly recommend them to you as well, as I believe they will make your journey even more enjoyable, as you will experience results quicker.

Write a journal

This one is my favorite and absolutely at the top. I have mentioned journaling briefly, but I have promised to reveal my practice of doing it.

I write a journal to reflect weekly what's happening in my life and my relationship. Let me point out my personal view on why you should be doing it as well:

- You reflect on your life.

Life moves quickly. Journaling offers you a great opportunity to stop and reflect on your life and your relationship.

- Journaling helps you understand.
  Writing things down about what's going on in your mind helps you develop a much better understanding of yourself and others, including your spouse.

- Journaling encourages gratitude. By keeping track of everything that you are grateful for, you become happier and more optimistic as you start enjoying the little things.

- Journaling is an emotional outlet. It helps you vent, but also gives you a clear perspective to forgive and move on.

- Journaling is a starting point for your inner peace. Journaling helps me turn my dreams into goals and goals into actions. It helps me stay focused, which gives me peace and stability.

Example of my weekly journaling routine

Every Sunday evening, I journal for about an hour. I do it digitally as this way my journal is always with me no matter where I am. I have developed a template with a set of questions that help lead my thoughts in the right direction.

- How was my week in general?

- What successes did I experience? What can I celebrate? What can I be proud of?
- Any magical moments? I put them in a separate folder called Magical Moments.
- What did I learn about myself?
- What did I learn about others?
- What do I plan to do differently or the same tomorrow?
- Who did I meet? What was interesting about them? Who will I follow up with? Anyone to send a note or thank you to?
- What are my top three goals that I want to accomplish NEXT week?

I put photos and videos at the end of each entry.

Remember the magical moments

It sounds simple and it is. Why is it then that so many people have an easier time remembering the bad stuff, while forgetting the good stuff? You should be doing exactly the opposite.

People who are happy are happy because they keep reminding themselves how happy they are.

Therefore, track and remember the magical moments of your time together and revisit those memories as often as you can!

There are a couple of ways of how you can do this. Let me share with you what I did for many years, and it works perfectly for me.

Hang your best photos on the wall. Find the best photos of both of you, as well as your best family photos. Have them professionally printed, frame them nicely and hang them on the walls of your house where you frequently pass by.

This is what will happen. After a week, your conscious mind won't notice the photos anymore, but your subconscious will. Each and every day your subconscious will get a message from the wall that says, "Life is good. We are having a great time together!"

Most of the photos will probably be from your family life. That is great, but don't forget to use a dedicated part of the wall just for the two of you.

Maybe you will want to combine these photos with your vision of your relationship as I do. My wife and I have twelve statements that form the core vision of our marriage. Accordingly, we have selected twelve photos that represent those statements and remind us of our core values of our relationship.

Remind yourself often

Establish your "Magical Moments" notebook and put your best photos and videos of your most previous moments together. Let them be moments when you were especially connected, relaxed and happy.

Then, when you are angry or annoyed with your partner, have a quick peek and watch what happens. Guaranteed, your mood will instantly get better as you'll remind yourself how lucky you actually are. It works for me, and you should try it as well.

It doesn't have to be photos or videos if you don't have them. It can be just a couple of lines or even a couple of words in your journal that remind you of certain magical occasions. Anything that will make you remember the good times will do.

Since it's one of the essential items to millions of people these days, I recommend using your phone for this purpose. It's simple because you can take, save and store your thoughts, images, photos and videos wherever you are and anytime you need. Otherwise, it might happen that you will simply forget, and that would be a shame.

Start exercising

Exercising will change your perspective, you will be more relaxed and you will feel better. As you feel better, you'll have a better relationship. This is backed up by extensive research, and it's also my personal experience. This can mean going to a gym regularly, but you can also run, walk or do anything that will get you moving your body, as long as it's not just typing on a keyboard like I am doing right now.

Take the time just for yourself

Don't forget about yourself. Pursue a hobby. Think about stuff that you've always wanted to do but "there wasn't enough time." For example, I enrolled in a music school, and I'm attending the same school as my son. He learns to play guitar and I do keyboards. It's great fun and it's something I always wanted to do. Beware though of doing your hobby excessively, and using it as an excuse for not spending time with your partner. Go out with your friends occasionally, visit museums, try something you always secretly wished for. Do something just for yourself. You will feel good and you'll be a happier person. Remember, not only will you feel better, but also people (including your spouse) like to hang out with happy people and avoid miserable ones. Think about that.

Afterword: What now?

No book can solve all relationship problems. If that was so easy, no one would have any problems in their relationship. I do expect though that by now you have a few more answers. The funny thing with marriage and intimate relationships is that we don't get a manual on our wedding day telling us how to get it right. We don't get all the information from our parents either. It's because they didn't have them or some of them were simply wrong.

That said, when writing this book, I didn't think I had all the answers. I still don't and neither will you. Anyone who claims they know it all is not telling you the truth. Human relationships are much too complex for that. Smart people learn and make mistakes until they die. I do expect, though, that, while reading this book and doing the exercises, you gained a better awareness of yourself and your spouse. By now you should be much better equipped to make your journey through life with your significant other a joyful one, experiencing bumps along the road only as an additional challenge and no longer as a danger to your relationship.

By following the principles of *Feel Good Marriage*, you can change the direction of your relationship for the better, and you can start changing it now. Don't think even for a second you have to apply all that is written in this book at once. You couldn't even if you wanted to. But it's also true that even the slightest change can have a big impact. The key is small, incremental steps each and every day. Just keep going.

If you are reading this, obviously, you had a lot of motivation to come to the end of the book. I thank you for your patience and congratulate you for your motivation. If you have read this book alone, without the participation of your partner, and you have decided to lead the way in changing your relationship for the better, I congratulate you for that as well. Only strong and confident people can do this.

I urge you, though, to have realistic expectations, especially time wise. You should expect, at first, that your partner might not respond to your attempts and changed behavior. That's because your partner might still be anticipating criticism, blame and other traits of your old behavior, and respond negatively. Don't give up now or fall prey to old behavior patterns that tell you to fight back and repeat the same old stuff again. Continue softly and gently, knowing that there will come a point in time when your spouse will also change his or her response. It may just take a while.

You WILL see the results, just don't expect them right away. It's like losing weight. You can of course enroll on some weird diet like having only bananas and milk for lunch for two weeks and lose some weight. But I bet if we fast-forward a couple of months, you will be back where you were, if not more so. Reality is, there are no quick fixes and the same is true for relationships. Be suspicious of anyone who tells you there are. You and your partner didn't get to this point overnight, so it will take some time and effort to get your relationship to its natural balance again.

Remember, ups and downs are okay, it means your relationship is alive and kicking! If there were no ups and downs, it would mean your relationship is dead.

There will be bad days when you'll think you didn't accomplish much. You will screw up and you'll be mad at yourself for doing so. Don't beat yourself up too much. Just say to yourself, *Tomorrow, I'll do better* (as I do), and learn from your mistakes, embrace them and move on.

After some quick successes, you might be tempted to back off a little. It's way too easy to resort back to old habits. Resist that temptation. Don't throw away what you have learned! Who knows, you might not have a second chance, and that would be a shame.

Make your new behaviors stick. Observe what's working well for you and create rituals, not just habits. Rituals are special, so is your relationship. Keep working on getting to know yourself and your partner better. Use disagreements to learn something new about yourself and your spouse.

Never lose faith. Never lose faith in yourself and never lose faith in your spouse and your relationship. Persist. The determination that you and your spouse show today directly influences what kind of marriage and relationship you will get tomorrow.

One of the last chapters in this book was about the vision and the purpose of your relationship. This is something worth pursuing. It's your North Star. Follow it, because your North Star will lead you no matter how many storms you go through. On your way, you'll discover it's more fun doing the journey than it is about the goal. You will discover that, while being on a journey together, practicing what this book is talking about, you've enjoyed the journey itself.

And you know something else? While transforming your relationship, you'll become a better person. You'll discover that you have changed. Not only will your spouse begin noticing, but other people will, as well. Your coworkers, friends and other people you know, WILL notice the difference. Finally, your children, if you have them or plan to have them, will be grateful to you, only they don't know it yet. If not sooner, they will be grateful when they engage in intimate relationships themselves with loving patterns that they learned from you, and as such, practically engraved in their subconscious to their advantage.

Finally, if this book has inspired you, do not withhold the information. Instead, I invite you to inspire others around you! Inspire the people that you love and the people that love you.

This way together, step-by-step, we will change the world for the better.

About the Author

Marko Petkovic is the author of the Amazon best-sellers the *Feel Good Marriage*, *47 Little Love Boosters For A Happy Marriage* and his latest book *The 5 Little Love Rituals*. He is also the founder of feelgoodrituals.com, dedicated to helping people achieve healthy, fulfilling relationships, personal success, and abundance. He believes that successful relationships are acts of doing, not having, and can therefore be learned. Marko believes that every person has a choice, and that everyone can change. From personal experience, he believes that most couples don't need marriage counseling, but just some education and guidance, and most of all, determination and a lot of practice.

Married for more than fifteen years, Marko writes for modern couples of the twenty-first century who struggle balancing their professional work with home and raising kids while trying to be good partners to their life mates.

Although Marko has managed to transform his own marriage into a fulfilling and healthy one, he didn't learn how to save a marriage in college. In fact, from his background, he holds master's degrees in engineering and economy. It was only later in his life when he found passion in applied psychology in which he is now licensed, studying how profoundly thoughts and feelings can affect human behavior.

He believes seemingly overwhelming problems can and should be broken down into simple, actionable steps that anyone can start implementing immediately. In that spirit, he strives for all of his work to be practical and down-to-earth, teaching only things that work and pass the test of common sense.

Marko is also the father of two boys. He would like to consider himself to be a kickass husband and father, but he still screws up every now and then. When this happens, he says to himself, *"Tomorrow, I'll do better,"* and sees those everyday family challenges as inspiration for his own work. He starts his day early and believes that hope is not a plan.

Last Thing

THANK YOU for purchasing this book!

So, if you've landed here and read up to this point then the only thing left is to do me a small favor.

See, online bookstores use reviews to rank books AND many readers like you evaluate the quality of a title based solely on the feedback from others.

To put it simply :) Reviews are kind of a big deal to authors like me!

So, of you have a minute or so to write a couple of words about the book (good or bad!) today, that would be great! It would mean a world to me.

You can even **leave your review anonymously** (or under a pen name) without revealing your real name.

To leave your review, visit one of the the links below:

Amazon: bit.ly/fgmreview

iTunes, Barnes & Noble, Kobo: bit.ly/fgmreviewother

Not sure how to write a review?

Here's a simple template that you can use.

- What did you like most/least about the book?

- What's your most important takeaway or insight from the book? Why is it important to you?

- What did or will you start doing differently because of the book?

- What would you change about the book?

- Who would you recommend the book to the most?

It doesn't have to be lengthy or professional!

THANK YOU!

You're awesome.

Get in Touch

If you'd like to get in touch with me please visit the link below.

Also, if you have an issue with accessing your bonus section, or you have some feedback, would like to work with me or simply chat, just pop me a message here:

http://geni.us/contactmarko

I'm looking forward to hearing from you!

Disclaimer Notice

The author made his best effort to provide accurate and authoritative information. Even though the author of this material is well conversed in the subject matter, the material contained in this book does not constitute professional advice. If professional assistance is required, the services of a competent professional should be sought.

All the material contained in this book is provided for educational and informational purposes only. No responsibility can be taken for any results or outcomes resulting from the use of this material.

While every attempt has been made to provide information that is both accurate and effective, the author does not assume any responsibility for the accuracy or use/misuse of this information.

Printed in Great Britain
by Amazon